GENERAL EDITOR: JAMES GIBSON

JANE AUSTEN	*Emma* No...
	Sense and Se...
	Persuasion ...y Simons
	Pride and Prejudice Raymond Wilson
	Mansfield Park Richard Wirdnam
SAMUEL BECKETT	*Waiting for Godot* Jennifer Birkett
WILLIAM BLAKE	*Songs of Innocence* and *Songs of Experience* Alan Tomlinson
ROBERT BOLT	*A Man for All Seasons* Leonard Smith
CHARLOTTE BRONTË	*Jane Eyre* Robert Miles
EMILY BRONTË	*Wuthering Heights* Hilda D. Spear
JOHN BUNYAN	*The Pilgrim's Progress* Beatrice Batson
GEOFFREY CHAUCER	*The Miller's Tale* Michael Alexander
	The Pardoner's Tale Geoffrey Lester
	The Wife of Bath's Tale Nicholas Marsh
	The Knight's Tale Anne Samson
	The Prologue to the Canterbury Tales Nigel Thomas and Richard Swan
JOSEPH CONRAD	*The Secret Agent* Andrew Mayne
CHARLES DICKENS	*Bleak House* Dennis Butts
	Great Expectations Dennis Butts
	Hard Times Norman Page
GEORGE ELIOT	*Middlemarch* Graham Handley
	Silas Marner Graham Handley
	The Mill on the Floss Helen Wheeler
T. S. ELIOT	*Murder in the Cathedral* Paul Lapworth
	Selected Poems Andrew Swarbrick
HENRY FIELDING	*Joseph Andrews* Trevor Johnson
E. M. FORSTER	*Howards End* Ian Milligan
	A Passage to India Hilda D. Spear
WILLIAM GOLDING	*The Spire* Rosemary Sumner
	Lord of the Flies Raymond Wilson
OLIVER GOLDSMITH	*She Stoops to Conquer* Paul Ranger
THOMAS HARDY	*The Mayor of Casterbridge* Ray Evans
	Tess of the d'Urbervilles James Gibson
	Far from the Madding Crowd Colin Temblett-Wood
GERARD MANLEY HOPKINS	*Selected Poems* John Garrett
BEN JONSON	*Volpone* Michael Stout
JOHN KEATS	*Selected Poems* John Garrett
RUDYARD KIPLING	*Kim* Leonée Ormond
PHILIP LARKIN	*The Whitsun Weddings* and *The Less Deceived* Andrew Swarbrick

MACMILLAN MASTER GUIDES

MACMILLAN MASTER GUIDES

TWELFTH NIGHT

BY WILLIAM SHAKESPEARE

R. P. DRAPER

with an Introduction by
HAROLD BROOKS

MACMILLAN
EDUCATION

First edition 1988

Published by
MACMILLAN EDUCATION LTD
Houndmills, Basingstoke, Hampshire RG21 2XS
and London
Companies and representatives
throughout the world

Printed in Hong Kong
Typeset by TecSet Ltd, Wallington, Surrey.

British Library Cataloguing in Publication Data
Draper, R. P. (Ronald Philip), *1928–*
Twelfth night by William Shakespeare.—
(Macmillan master guides).
1. Drama in English Shakespeare, William.
Twelfth night. Critical Studies
I. Title   II. Shakespeare, William,
1564–1616   Twelfth night
822.3′3
ISBN 0–333–37202–6 Pbk
ISBN 0–333–39468–2 Pbk export

CONTENTS

GENERAL EDITOR'S PREFACE

The aim of the Macmillan Master Guides is to help you to appreciate the book you are studying by providing information about it and by suggesting ways of reading and thinking about it which will lead to a fuller understanding. The section on the writer's life and background has been designed to illustrate those aspects of the writer's life which have influenced the work, and to place it in its personal and literary context. The summaries and critical commentary are of special importance in that each brief summary of the action is followed by an examination of the significant critical points. The space which might have been given to repetitive explanatory notes has been devoted to a detailed analysis of the kind of passage which might confront you in an examination. Literary criticism is concerned with both the broader aspects of the work being studied and with its detail. The ideas which meet us in reading a great work of literature, and their relevance to us today, are an essential part of our study, and our Guides look at the thought of their subject in some detail. But just as essential is the craft with which the writer has constructed his work of art, and this may be considered under several technical headings – characterisation, language, style and stagecraft, for example.

The authors of these Guides are all teachers and writers of wide experience, and they have chosen to write about books they admire and know well in the belief that they can communicate their admiration to you. But you yourself must read and know intimately the book you are studying. No one can do that for you. You should see this book as a lamp-post. Use it to shed light, not to lean against. If you know your text and know what it is saying about life, and how it says it, then you will enjoy it, and there is no better way of passing an examination in literature.

JAMES GIBSON

AN INTRODUCTION TO THE STUDY OF SHAKESPEARE'S PLAYS

A play as a work of art exists to the full only when performed. It must hold the audience's attention throughout the performance, and, unlike a novel, it can't be put down and taken up again. It is important to experience the play as if you are seeing it on the stage for the first time, and you should begin by reading it straight through. Shakespeare builds a play in dramatic units which may be divided into smaller subdivisions, or episodes, marked off by exits and entrances and lasting as long as the same actors are on the stage. Study it unit by unit.

The first unit provides the exposition which is designed to put the audience into the picture. In the second unit we see the forward movement of the play as one situation changes into another. The last unit in a tragedy or a tragical play will bring the catastrophe, and in comedy – and some of the history plays – an unravelling of the complications, what is called a *dénouement*.

The onward movement of the play from start to finish is its progressive structure. We see the chain of cause and effect (the plot) and the progressive revelation and development of character. The people, their characters and their motives drive the plot forward in a series of scenes which are carefully planned to give variety of pace and excitement. We notice fast-moving and slower-moving episodes, tension mounting and slackening, and alternative fear and hope for the characters we favour. Full-stage scenes, such as stately councils and processions or turbulent mobs, contrast with scenes of small groups or even single speakers. Each of the scenes presents a deed or event which changes the situation. In performances, entrances and exits and stage actions are physical facts, with more impact than on the page. That impact Shakespeare relied upon, and we must restore it by an effort of the imagination.

Shakespeare's language is just as diverse. Quickfire dialogue is followed by long speeches, and verse changes to prose. There is a wide range of speech — formal, colloquial, dialect, 'Mummerset' and the broken English of foreigners, for example. Songs, instrumental music, and the noise of battle, revelry and tempest, all extend the range of dramatic expression. The dramatic use of language is enhanced by skilful stagecraft, by costumes, by properties such as beds, swords and Yorick's skull, by such stage business as kneeling, embracing and giving money, and by use of such features of the stage structure as the balcony and the trapdoor.

By these means Shakespeare's people are brought vividly to life and cleverly individualised. But though they have much to tell us about human nature, we must never forget that they are characters in a play, not in real life. And remember, they exist to enact the play, not the play to portray *them*.

Shakespeare groups his characters so that they form a pattern, and it is useful to draw a diagram showing this. Sometimes a linking character has dealings with each group. The pattern of persons belongs to the symmetric structure of the play, and its dramatic unity is reinforced and enriched by a pattern of resemblances and contrasts; for instance, between characters, scenes, recurrent kinds of imagery, and words. It is not enough just to notice a feature that belongs to the symmetric structure, you should ask what its relevance is to the play as a whole and to the play's ideas.

These ideas and the dramatising of them in a central theme, or several related to each other, are a principal source of the dramatic unity. In order to see what themes are present and important, look, as before, for pattern. Observe the place in it of the leading character. In tragedy this will be the protagonist, in comedy heroes and heroines, together with those in conflict or contrast with them. In *Henry IV Part I,* Prince Hal is being educated for kingship and has a correct estimate of honour, while Falstaff despises honour, and Hotspur makes an idol of it. Pick out the episodes of great intensity as, for example, in *King Lear* where the theme of spiritual blindness is objectified in the blinding of Gloucester, and similarly, note the emphases given by dramatic poetry as in Prospero's 'Our revels now are ended . . .'or unforgettable utterances such as Lear's 'Is there any cause in Nature that makes these hard hearts?' Striking stage-pictures such as that of Hamlet behind the King at prayer will point to leading themes, as will all the parallels and recurrences, including those of phrase and imagery. See whether, in the play you are studying, themes known to be favourites with Shakespeare are prominent, themes such as those of order and dis-order, relationships disrupted by mistakes about identity, and appearance and reality. The latter were bound to fascinate Shakespeare, whose theatrical art worked by means of illusions which pointed beyond the surface of actual life to underlying truths. In looking at themes beware of attempts to make the play fit some orthodoxy a critic believes in — Freudian perhaps, or Marxist, or dogmatic Christian theology — and remember that its ideas, though they often have a bearing on ours, are Elizabethan.

Some of Shakespeare's greatness lies in the good parts he wrote for the actors. In his demands upon them, and the opportunities he provided, he bore their professional skills in mind and made use of their physical prowess, relished by a public accustomed to judge fencing and wrestling as expertly as we today judge football and tennis. As a member of the professional group of players called the Chamberlain's Men he knew each actor he was writing for. To play his women he had highly trained boys. As paired heroines they were often contrasted, short with tall, for example, or one vivacious and enterprising, the other more conventionally feminine.

Richard Burbage, the company's leading man, was famous as a great tragic actor, and he took leading roles in seven of Shakespeare's *tragedies*. Though each of the seven has its own distinctiveness, we shall find at the centre of all of them a tragic protagonist possessing tragic greatness, not just one 'tragic flaw' but a tragic vulnerability. He will have a character which makes him unfit to cope with the tragic situations confronting him, so that his tragic errors bring down upon him tragic suffering and finally a tragic catastrophe. Normally, both the suffering and the catastrophe are far worse than he can be said to deserve, and others are engulfed in them who deserve such a fate less or not at all. Tragic terror is aroused in us because, though exceptional, he is sufficiently near to normal humankind for his fate to remind us of what can happen to human beings like ourselves, and because we see in it a combination of inexorable law and painful mystery. We recognise the principle of cause and effect where in a tragic world errors return upon those who make them, but we are also aware of the tragic disproportion between cause and effect. In a tragic world you may kick a stone and start an avalanche which will destroy you and others with you. Tragic pity is aroused in us by this disproportionate suffering, and also by all the kinds of suffering undergone by every character who has won our imaginative sympathy. Imaginative sympathy is wider than moral approval, and is felt even if suffering does seem a just and logical outcome. In addition to pity and terror we have a sense of tragic waste because catastrophe has affected so much that was great and fine. Yet we feel also a tragic exaltation. To our grief the men and women who represented those values have been destroyed, but the values themselves have been shown not to depend upon success, nor upon immunity from the worst of tragic sufferings and disaster.

Comedies have been of two main kinds, or cross-bred from the two. In critical comedies the governing aim is to bring out the absurdity or irrationality of follies and abuses, and make us laugh at them. Shakespeare's comedies often do this, but most of them belong primarily to the other kind – romantic comedy. Part of the romantic appeal is to our liking for suspense; they are dramas of averted threat, beginning in trouble and ending in joy. They appeal to the romantic senses of adventure and of wonder, and to complain that they are improbable is silly because the improbability, the marvellousness, is part of the pleasure. They dramatise stories of romantic love, accompanied by love doctrine – ideas and ideals of love. But they are plays in two tones, they are comic as well as romantic. There is often something to laugh at even in the love stories of the nobility and gentry, and just as there is high comedy in such incidents as the cross-purposes of the young Athenians in the wood, and Rosalind as 'Ganymede' teasing Orlando, there is always broad comedy for characters of lower rank. Even where one of the sub-plots has no effect on the main plot, it may take up a topic from it and present it in a more comic way.

What is there in the play to make us laugh or smile? We can distinguish many kinds of comedy it may employ. *Language* can amuse by its wit, or by absurdity, as in Bottom's malapropisms. Feste's nonsense-phrases, so fatuously admired by Sir Andrew, are deliberate, while his catechising of Olivia is clown-routine. Ass-headed Bottom embraced by the Fairy Queen is a *comic spectacle* combining costume and stage-business. His wanting to play every part is *comedy of character*. Phebe disdaining Silvius and in love with 'Ganymede', or Malvolio treating Olivia as though she had written him a love-letter is *comedy of situation*; the situation is laughably different from what Phebe or Malvolio supposes. A comic let-down or anticlimax can be devastating, as we see when Aragon, sure that he deserves Portia, chooses the silver casket only to find the portrait not of her but of a 'blinking idiot'. By *slapstick, caricature* or sheer *ridiculousness of situation*, comedy can be exaggerated into farce, which Shakespeare knows how to use on occasion. At the opposite extreme, before he averts the threat, he can carry it to the brink of tragedy, but always under control.

Dramatic irony is the result of a character or the audience anticipating an outcome which, comically or tragically, turns out very differently. Sometimes *we* foresee that it will. The speaker never foresees how ironical, looking back, the words or expectations will appear. When she says, 'A little water clears us of this deed,' Lady Macbeth has no prevision of her sleep-walking words, 'Will these hands ne'er be clean?' There is irony in the way in which in all Shakespeare's tragic plays except *Richard II* comedy is found in the very heart of the tragedy. The Porter scene in *Macbeth* comes straight after Duncan's murder. In *Hamlet* and *Antony and Cleopatra* comic episodes lead into the catastrophe: the rustic Countryman brings Cleopatra the means of death, and the satirised Osric departs with Hamlet's assent to the fatal fencing match. The Porter, the Countryman and Osric are not mere 'comic relief', they contrast with the tragedy in a way that adds something to it, and affects our response.

A sense of the comic and the tragic is common ground between Shakespeare and his audience. Understandings shared with the audience are necessary to all drama. They include conventions, i.e. assumptions, contrary to what factual realism would demand, which the audience silently agrees to accept. It is, after all, by a convention, what Coleridge called a 'willing suspension of disbelief', that an actor is accepted as Hamlet. We should let a play teach us the conventions it depends on. Shakespeare's conventions allow him to take a good many liberties, and he never troubles about inconsistencies that wouldn't trouble an audience. What matters to the dramatist is the effect he creates. So long as we are responding as he would wish, Shakespeare would not care whether we could say by what means he has made us do so. But to appreciate his skill, and get a fuller understanding of his play, we have to distinguish these means, and find terms to describe them.

If you approach the Shakespeare play you are studying bearing in mind what is said to you here, then you will respond to it more fully than before. Yet like all works of artistic genius, Shakespeare's can only be analysed so far. His drama and its poetry will always have about them something 'which into words no critic can digest'.

HAROLD BROOKS

ACKNOWLEDGEMENT

Cover illustration: *Twelfth Night, 1850* by Walter Howard Deverell, from the Forbes Magazine Collection, New York, and by courtesy of the Bridgeman Art Library.

1 SHAKESPEARE'S LIFE AND THE BACKGROUND TO *TWELFTH NIGHT*

Shakespeare was born at Stratford-upon-Avon in 1564. He was baptised on 26 April, and the tradition has grown up that he was born on St George's Day, i.e. 23 April; but there is no evidence for this. John Shakespeare, his father, was a prominent businessman in Stratford, who rose to the position of high bailiff (or mayor) in 1568, but who later fell into debt, possibly through having to pay heavy fines imposed on him as a Roman Catholic. His mother, Mary Arden, was of higher social standing than her husband, being the daughter of a gentleman landowner from Wilmcote, near Stratford.

Comparatively little is known of Shakespeare's early years. It is likely that he was educated at King's New School, the grammar school in Stratford, where he acquired the 'small Latin and less Greek' rather disparagingly attributed to him by the contemporary playwright and poet, Ben Jonson – though 'small' by Jonson's standards may have been considerable enough by those of less learned men than he. There is probably little truth in the legend that he poached deer in Sir Thomas Lucy's park at Charlecote; and John Aubrey's tale of his being apprenticed to a butcher is equally doubtful, though it is embroidered with the attractive suggestion that 'when he kill'd a calfe, he would doe it in high style, and make a speech'.

In November 1582, when Shakespeare was 18, a licence was issued for his marriage to Anne Hathaway, the daughter of Richard Hathaway of Hewlands Farm, Shottery, on the outskirts of Stratford. She was eight years his senior, and since their first child, Susanna, was christened on 26 May 1583 it may be that the wedding was forced on Shakespeare. Several commentators have suggested that the advice given to 'Cesario' in *Twelfth Night* not to take a wife older than himself is based on the dramatist's own experience, and the fact that he spent so much time apart from Anne in London seems to point to their marriage as having been a failure. This is speculation, however. What is known is that twins (a boy named Hamnet and a girl named Judith) were born in 1585, and that Shakespeare took care to provide for both them and his wife. The notorious bequest, made to Anne in his will – 'Item, I give unto my wife my second best bed with the furniture' – has often been cited as evidence of their estrangement, but Schoenbaum notes that 'a widow may have been entitled by custom to one-third of her husband's estate, and that there was therefore no need to mention this disposition in the will' (*The Cambridge Companion to Shakespeare Studies*, p. 11).

At some point in the 1580s Shakespeare left Stratford for London and began his career as an actor–playwright, first with the company known as Lord Pembroke's Men and then with the Lord Chamberlain's Men. The latter soon established itself as the leading theatre company in London, thanks in no small degree to the plays which Shakespeare began to write for it, and on the accession of James I to the throne of England it was honoured with the title of the King's Men. Shakespeare's earliest plays were probably the histories, *Henry VI* Parts 1, 2 and 3, *Richard III* and *King John*; the tragedy of *Titus Andronicus*; and the three comedies, *The Comedy of Errors*, *The Taming of the Shrew* and *The Two Gentlemen of Verona* – all of which are assigned by Peter Alexander, in his *Complete Works of Shakespeare*, to the period 1584–92. He had certainly achieved enough of a reputation by 1592 to attract the jealous attention of Robert Greene – one of the so-called 'University wits' who had hitherto been the chief purveyor of dramatic scripts for the rapidly developing theatres of the Elizabethan period. In his pamphlet, *Greenes Groatsworth of Wit*, written on his deathbed, Greene warns his fellow dramatists (men like Peele, Kyd and Marlowe) not to trust the actors any longer, especially as there is among them 'an upstart Crow, beautified with our feathers, that with his *Tygers hart wrapt in a Players hyde*, supposes he is as well able to bombast out a blanke verse as the best of you: and being an absolute *Iohannes fac totum* [Jack-of-all-trades], is in his owne conceit the onely Shake-scene in a countrey'. The pun on 'Shake-scene' and the allusion to *Henry VI, Part 3* (York inveighs against the unfeminine Queen Margaret, who domineers over her peaceable husband, Henry VI, with the line, 'O tiger's heart wrapp'd in a woman's hide', I.iv.137) point clearly to the young William Shakespeare, who has the temerity, despite the fact that he is merely an uneducated player, to write plays which he – and, no doubt, the theatre audience as well – considers every bit as good as those by the established authors.

This attack was quickly rebutted by Henry Chettle, who wrote in the 'Epistle' to his *Kind-Harts Dreame* (1592) that he had himself seen the man in question 'no lesse civill' in his demeanour 'than he exelent in the qualitie he professes' – a reference, it would seem, to Shakespeare's skill as an actor; and he adds that 'divers of worship have reported his uprightness of dealing, which argues his honesty, and his facetious grace in writting, that aproves his Art'. Tradition has it that Shakespeare played Adam in *As You Like It* and was particularly good in kingly parts, including the ghost of Old Hamlet in *Hamlet*. But he seems to have become the business man of his Company rather than an actor and, increasingly, their most successful author, producing plays at an average rate of two per year.

There was an interruption of theatrical activity in 1592–4 owing to the plague, and during this time Shakespeare turned his attention to narrative rather than dramatic poetry, publishing the love poem, *Venus and Adonis*, in 1593 and the more tragic *The Rape of Lucrece* in 1594 (though the play *Love's Labour's Lost* probably also belongs to this period). From 1594 to 1599, however, he wrote ten plays, including *Romeo and Juliet*, the four histories covering the reigns of Richard II, Henry IV and Henry V, and such brilliant comedies as *A Midsummer Night's Dream*, *The Merchant of Venice*, *Much Ado About Nothing* and *As You Like It*. His sonnets were not published until 1609, but most of these were also written in the 1590s, when Shakespeare's mind seems to have been most preoccupied with the theme of love.

Twelfth Night is the last in this sequence of comedies. Its precise date is claimed by Leslie Hotson in his ingenious reconstruction, *The First Night of 'Twelfth Night'* (1954), to be 6 January (i.e. the night of Twelfth Night) 1601. Hotson's case is based on the assumption that a play, known to have been performed by the Lord Chamberlain's Men in the Great Chamber at Whitehall Palace at the end of the Christmas period 1600–1, was Shakespeare's appropriately titled *Twelfth Night*. The particular occasion for this 'royal command performance' was Queen Elizabeth's entertainment of a handsome young Italian suitor, Orsino, Duke of Bracciano; and Hotson seeks to support his theory by showing that it provides the key to a whole series of topical elements within the play, including the satire on Sir William Knollys, Comptroller of the Queen's household, on whom the character of Malvolio is supposedly based. Sir William's father, Sir Francis Knollys, was a well-known supporter of the Puritans; Sir William himself had a ridiculous infatuation with a pretty Maid of Honour, Mary (or 'Mal') Fitton, much younger than himself, who, ironically, became pregnant by another man; and it is further suggested that the name 'Malvolio', is a pun on *Mal-voglio* (= 'I want Mal'). However, more recent commentators are not convinced; they regard the evidence as inconclusive, and consider that it is inherently unlikely that Queen Elizabeth would have allowed Orsino's name to be used in this way. It is possible that *recollection* of the Duke's visit may have influenced Shakespeare when he composed the play at a later date, and this may also explain the choice of name for his Duke.

The first recorded reference to a production of *Twelfth Night* is in the diary of John Manningham, a law student in the Middle Temple, who, on 2 February 1602 made the following entry:

At our feast wee had a play called 'Twelve Night, or What You Will', much like the Commedy of Errores, or Menechmi in Plautus, but most like and neere to that in Italian called *Inganni*. A good practise in it to make the Steward beleeve his Lady widdowe was in love with him, by counterfeyting a letter as from his Lady in generall termes, telling him what she liked best in him, and prescribing his gesture in smiling, his apparaile, &c., and then when he came to practise making him beleeve they tooke him to be mad. (Quoted by E. K. Chambers, *A Short Life of Shakespeare*, p. 177)

This indicates that the play was in existence by the early part of 1602 and is not incompatible with the general idea that Christmas-time festivity was in Shakespeare's mind; but it is doubtful whether the play was both written and produced by the date necessitated for Hotson's 'first night'.

If *Twelfth Night* is, as many readers and theatre-goers would affirm, the best of Shakespeare's 'mature' comedies, it is also the one which includes the most elements of sadness as well, and it is not without significance that it overlaps in date with the sequence of tragedies which represents Shakespeare's most profound and disturbingly original contribution to English drama: *Julius Caesar* (1599), *Hamlet* (1600-1), and *Othello*, *Timon of Athens*, *King Lear*, *Macbeth*, *Antony and Cleopatra* and *Coriolanus* – all written in the period 1601-8.

Moreover, the other plays of this astonishingly productive period – *Troilus and Cressida*, *Measure for Measure* and *All's Well That Ends Well* – though nominally 'comedies', are so darkened with satirical bitterness and potentially tragic characters and situations that they are acknowledged to belong to a 'problem' category which is more akin to that of the tragedies proper. During this decade for whatever reason (and the lack of anything but the scantiest factual evidence compels one to speculations which are necessarily based on subjective impressions of the plays themselves) Shakespeare seems to have experienced a crisis of disillusionment and to have poured his feelings of horror at the cruelty and ingratitude of which human beings are capable into poetic and dramatic forms which are strained almost to breaking point. The intensity seems at times unbearable, and the intuition of pain and suffering beyond what the imagination can accommodate. And yet at the same time there is also a powerful sense of creative energy responding sublimely to the challenge and triumphantly converting the experience into new linguistic and theatrical art.

The texts of these plays are in some instances so long and their speculative range so great that the possiblities of actual performance seem to be outstripped. It is almost certain, for example, that the full-length *Hamlet* of modern editions was not produced in Shakespeare's own time. Nevertheless it is a mistake to under-estimate his commitment to the theatre. He wrote specifically for the company of actors to which he belonged, and with the requirements of the Elizabethan stage in the forefront of his mind. During the period of his most vigorous output he also lived and worked in London, occupying lodgings close to the theatres on which his professional life was centred, and his closest friends were fellow actors, such as Heminge and Condell, who edited his plays in the first 'Folio' edition after his death. (Shakespeare himself seems to have been indifferent to publication).

However, Shakespeare did not sever his connection with Stratford. His father, John Shakespeare, had attempted to gain the right to a coat of arms – the sign of acceptance as a gentleman in Elizabethan England – but had failed. In 1596 the cause was taken up again by his son, who was successful this time; and in 1597 he bought the house in Stratford called 'New Place', which became his family dwelling. Shakespeare purchased other properties in Stratford during the early years of the new century, and he was also involved in lawsuits there. While still living in London he made various visits to his native town, but from about 1610 he made Stratford his permanent home once more, returning to London as and when his theatrical business required.

Among these occasions would, no doubt, have been the perfor-mance of his so-called 'last plays' – *Pericles*, *Cymbeline*, *The Winter's Tale* and *The Tempest* – belonging to the period 1608–13. These plays show a revival of interest in comedy and romance (they are some-times called 'the late romances') but with a new, tragi-comic em-phasis on catastrophic events which bring their characters to the brink of disasters from which, however, they are finally rescued. There is also a marked emphasis on the relations between parents and children and on the intervention of divinity in human affairs, suggesting a certain mellowing of Shakespeare's outlook and the development of a quasi-religious vision which includes new hope and faith in a restorative power associated with offspring and the innocence of youth.

Shakespeare's life was now drawing towards its end. His very last work, *Henry VIII*, written in collaboration with John Fletcher, was performed in 1613 – the year in which the Globe Theatre was burnt down. In January 1616 (or possibly 1615) he made his will, leaving bequests to various members of his family and to friends, but the bulk of his estate to his eldest daughter, Susanna. He died on 23 April 1616, and was buried at Holy Trinity church, Stratford.

2 SUMMARY
AND
CRITICAL COMMENTARY*

Act 1, Scene 1

Orsino, Duke of Illyria, listens to music. He receives news that his suit to the Countess Olivia has been rejected, and that she intends to isolate herself and mourn her dead brother for seven years.

This brief scene is a highly atmospheric one. It introduces the lovesick Orsino, and also suggests something about the sentimental and consuming nature of his love. Music is for him a form of aesthetic indulgence: the piece to which he is listening is beautifully cadenced (has 'a dying fall') but leads to weariness. And love, though 'quick' and 'fresh' ('Keen' and 'hungry', but with the word 'quick' also connoting 'life', as in the phrase, 'the quick and the dead'), has a similarly reductive effect. It is characterised by idle playfulness – hence the appropriately banal pun on 'hart/heart', but it has a savagely negative undertone, as hinted by the simile in which Orsino's 'desires' are likened to hunting dogs (with a reminiscence of the well-known tale of Actaeon, who was transformed to a stag and torn to pieces by his own hounds because he saw the goddess Diana naked). The language in which the messenger, Valentine, tells of Olivia's rejection of Orsino's suit is equally self-conscious, as is Orsino's reaction at lines 33–41. The whole scene creates a sense of pleasingly luxuriant verbal artifice which is nevertheless overdone; it is romantic, yet slightly suspect.

Act I, Scene ii

Viola, who has been shipwrecked on the coast of Illyria, enquires from a Captain where she is. She believes that her brother is

* The text used throughout this commentary is that of the Macmillan Shakespeare *Twelfth Night*, edited by E. A. J. Honigmann.

drowned, though she is given some hope that he may have survived. She learns about Orsino and about Olivia's grief for her brother, and she resolves to serve Orsino in disguise.

The main purpose of this scene is to provide the audience with information and set up Viola's disguise situation. In the process, however, the themes of tragedy and comedy are both adumbrated. Storm, a frequent symbol in Shakespeare for tragedy, gives way to survival and hope; but the uncertainty of life is emphasised – for example, by the play on the words 'chance' and 'perchance' (= 'per-haps', but also 'through [Latin *per*] chance') at lines 4–7. Neverthe-less, the Captain's account of how Viola's brother (Sebastian, but as yet unnamed) bound himself to a mast creates a strong image of resourcefulness, and Viola, though at the mercy of chance, is quick to size up her situation and devise a scheme for dealing with it. Critics differ as to whether she is also quick to see the possibility of a future husband in the shape of Orsino. It is easy to read too much significance into 'He was a bachelor then' (28), which, at this stage, is probably merely informative. Viola's attitude is essentially one of cautious optimism; she will put herself in a position to take advantage of what may come her way, but she knows that her power to control events is strictly limited: 'What else may hap to time I will commit' (58).

Act I, Scene iii

Olivia's uncle, Sir Toby Belch, is warned by Maria, her waiting-gentlewoman, that his drunken behaviour will get him into trouble. His friend, and dupe, Sir Andrew Aguecheek, makes his entrance, and complains that Olivia, whom he is trying to woo, ignores him. He declares his intention to go away, but is persuaded to continue his suit.

Unlike the previous ones, this scene is in prose, as befits the low-life characters of Sir Toby, Sir Andrew and Maria. The theme of wooing provides both continuity and contrast with what has gone before: Sir Andrew is another would-be suitor for Olivia's hand and provides a burlesque version of Orsino's wooing. In the main, however, this is a scene of farcical comedy, full of references to drinking and dancing, and the relationship between Sir Andrew and Sir Toby is that of gull and guller (Sir Toby deceives Sir Andrew into thinking that he has hopes of winning Olivia in order to make fun of him and to relieve him of his money). It is a foil to the romantic love comedy that we have seen up to now; and in so far as we see Sir Andrew in action as a lover, it is *vis à vis* Maria rather than

Olivia – his attempts to 'accost' Maria being thwarted by her greater realism and sharpness of wit.

Act I, Scene iv

Viola, now disguised as a boy, with the adopted name of 'Cesario', has already won favour with Orsino, who sends her as his proxy wooer to Olivia.

The plot moves on rapidly. In her disguise Viola is commissioned to plead Orsino's love suit, yet, as we learn in the concluding, poignant couplet, this has already created for her 'a barful strife' (a conflict involving many barriers) since, as she puts it, 'Whoe'er I woo, myself would be his wife.' At the same time Shakespeare is making theatrical capital, as he had previously done in comedies like *The Two Gentlemen of Verona*, *The Merchant of Venice* and *As You Like It*, out of the situation in which a heroine, who is in fact being played by a boy actor, takes on the appearance and manners of a young man. She thus enjoys the greater freedom for action which is the privilege of the male, while retaining the consciousness, and many of the attributes, of the female. (For example, see lines 32–8, where Orsino insists on the smoothness and ruddiness of Cesario's lips, 'his' treble voice and all being 'semblative a woman's part'). The emotional effect is also intensified, and the dramatic tension further heightened, by the audience's ability to share Viola's feelings, and savour the complexity of her situation, in a way that the characters on stage can not.

Act I, Scene v

Feste, Olivia's Fool, is introduced, in conversation with Maria. He seems to have been absent without leave. After some banter between him and Olivia and her steward, Malvolio, we learn that Viola/Cesario is demanding entrance at the gate. Olivia relents and agrees to hear this new messenger alone. She is so taken with Cesario's eloquence and youthful good looks that when the interview is over she sends Malvolio after 'him' with a ring which Cesario is supposed to have left behind, but which is merely a pretext for getting 'him' to return at a later time.

The previous scene was mainly in verse. With the opening of this scene, however, there is a return to prose, which is appropriate not only to Feste's social station, but also to his jesting, which is of a deliberately debunking nature. This is particularly apparent in the exchange between Feste and Olivia, where the servant has the temerity to 'prove' his mistress a fool – first, briefly, and by implication only (39–40), and then formally, and more extensively, in the 'catechism' (i.e. question and answer) of lines 59–73. Although this is an example of the set-piece demonstration of wit expected of a professional Fool, and as such need not be taken too seriously (the wrong way of responding to it is acted out for us by the ill-tempered comment of Malvolio: 'I marvel your ladyship takes delight in such a barren rascal . . . ', 84–91), there is nonetheless a meaningful connection to be made with the criticism of false sentiment which has already begun to emerge. Olivia's love for her brother is extravagant when it blinds her to the reality of the here-and-now. She is, indeed, an emotional 'fool' to overdo grief and mourning in such fashion. This is also interestingly associated with criticism of another kind of falsification of 'love' when Olivia rebukes Malvolio for being 'sick of self-love' (91). And authority is given to both examples of the criticism of false sentiment by Olivia's defence of the 'allowed [licensed] fool'.

Another effect of such criticism is to build a bridge to the second half of the scene, in which Olivia reveals a surprising inconsistency in allowing Cesario into her presence despite the fact that she has hitherto been adamant in refusing to receive any more messengers from Orsino. Malvolio's account of Viola/Cesario's stubbornness begins to intrigue Olivia, and though she makes a show of ticking off this impertinent youngster for 'sauciness' she does not cut 'him' off, but gives 'him' more and more scope. With striking dramatic effect (especially for an Elizabethan audience, who had more of an ear for such things than a modern audience) there is also a change from prose to verse shortly after the two characters are left alone. Their intimacy is dangerously emotional, and the whole temperature of the language is raised, heating up to more than conventional 'sighs of fire' (159) when Viola describes how, if she were in love with Olivia, she would 'Make me a willow cabin at your gate . . . ' (171–9). The speech is one that Olivia finds very moving; and its effect is adroitly indicated by Shakespeare, not by giving an equivalently poetic and resonant reply to Olivia, but by causing her to murmur the simple yet telling, understatement: 'You might do much'. These few words reveal significant change in Olivia: she is almost too much moved to speak, and when she does go on to repeat her refusal of Orsino's suit she is both laconic ('I cannot love him. Let him send no more') and almost self-contradictory – virtually taking back what she has just said ('Unless, perchance, you come to me again'). She seems to have lost the dignity and self-control of a high-born lady; and she even makes the social blunder of trying to tip Viola (who crisply retorts: 'I

am no fee'd post, lady'). After Viola's exit we get a dramatically
fluctuating soliloquy from Olivia (292–301) in which she broods on
the new messenger's physical attractions and catches herself in the act
of falling in love ('How now?/Even so quickly may one catch the
plague?'). Moreover, the action which follows speaks louder than
words: Olivia's transparent device of the ring to get the fascinating
messenger to come back again shows unconscious forces taking over.
As Olivia admits (to the audience, that is) 'I do I know not what'. She
loses self-control and surrenders to Fate:

Fate, show thy force; ourselves we do not owe [own],
What is decreed must be, and be this so. (313–14)

Act II, Scene i

Viola's twin brother, Sebastian, makes his appearance. He has been
saved from drowning by a sea-captain, Antonio, who has taken such
a liking to the young man that he begs to accompany him, but
Sebastian, though full of gratitude, refuses. He is bound for Orsino's
court; Antonio has many enemies there, but will follow Sebastian
nevertheless.
  This is a brief scene, which mainly forwards the plot. Stylistically,
its most prominent feature is the passage in which elaborately polite
expressions of regard are exchanged between Antonio and Sebastian.
This may seem extravagant for so short an acquaintance, but it is
probably to be accepted as a convention indicating the depth of their
friendship.

Act II, Scene ii

Malvolio pursues Viola to return the ring which she supposedly left
with Olivia. Viola realises that it is a device invented by Olivia
because she has fallen in love with the 'Cesario' persona.
  A favourite situation in romance has now been created: *A* loves *B*,
B loves *C*, *C* loves *A* (i.e. Orsino loves Olivia, Olivia loves 'Cesario',
'Cesario' – in reality Viola – loves Orsino). Disguise adds to the
complication to such an extent that in her soliloquy Viola calls it a
'wickedness' (27), and although she is an active heroine, rather than a
woman of 'waxen' heart easily deceived (as she suggests at lines
29–30), her plight and that of Olivia seem to her something over
which she has no control. It must be left to time to resolve – thus

creating a sense of uncertainty and apprehension which greatly enhances the dramatic tension of romantic comedy.

Act II, Scene iii

Sir Toby, Sir Andrew and Feste make merry late into the night. Maria warns them that their noise will offend Olivia, and Malvolio comes in to rebuke them on his lady's behalf. Maria sketches a plan for taking revenge on Malvolio by dropping a letter in his path which will lead him to think that Olivia is in love with him.

This is a scene of festivity which shows the boon-companion side of Sir Toby and his appreciation of Maria's wit (and which also provides an opportunity for Feste to sing one of his more attractive love-songs); but it also shows the riotously disorderly nature of Sir Toby's and Sir Andrew's behaviour. Malvolio has a point when he rebukes them for gabbling 'like tinkers at this time of night' (91) – a point underlined by the fact that Maria had already warned them for their 'caterwauling' (74). However, Malvolio makes himself very objectionable by his manner, and he shows great presumption in speaking as he does to Sir Toby, when he himself is but a steward and Sir Toby is 'consanguineous' (79) – i.e. a blood-relation of Olivia. Sir Andrew, on the other hand, though Malvolio's social superior, is incapable of living up to his knightly status, and commits the social solecism of suggesting that he might challenge Malvolio to a duel – though, with typical cowardice, not until *after* Malvolio has made his exit. The truth is that Malvolio and Sir Andrew are both fools in their different ways, and destined to be duped. Sir Andrew is already being gulled, and now a plan is afoot to gull Malvolio also. But Malvolio in particular seems to ask for what he is about to get; in the spirit of 'Twelfth Night' festivity his censorious attitude, with its 'Puritan' overtones, is made to compare badly with the 'cakes and ale' of Sir Toby, and there is no doubt whose side the audience is invited to take. Sir Toby stands for pleasure and relaxation. Malvolio (his very names suggests 'ill will') is a bad-tempered kill-joy. Nevertheless, it is highly characteristic of Shakespearian comedy that Sir Toby is not allowed to have everything his own way. Because of the shameless manner in which he lures Sir Andrew on, and the quite explicit criticism which is made of his drunken behaviour, he, too, shares some of the audience's disapproval. We warm to him and are wary of him at the same time. Moreover, we are not without some slight sympathy for Malvolio – and perhaps rather more for poor put-upon Sir Andrew.

Act II, Scene iv

Feste sings a love-song. Orsino discusses love with Viola/Cesario, and then dispatches 'him' yet again as a messenger to Olivia.

The whole of this scene is in verse, marking it as of greater emotional intensity and seriousness than the one that has gone before. To some extent it is a repetition of I.i, showing Orsino yet again as a rather sentimental character. He seems typically inconsistent in first admitting that men's affections are less stable than women's (32–5) but later on claiming that no woman is capable of so strong a passion as he feels for Olivia and that woman's love is inherently fickle (93–104); but, of course, the context varies – in the first instance Orsino is thinking of the need for a man to marry a woman younger than himself, while in the second he is seeking to rebut Viola/Cesario's argument that he might have to accept denial from Olivia, just as some woman, who might be in love with him, would have to live with the unpleasant reality of his inability to love her.

Feste probably voices the attitude expected of the audience when, with rather surprising boldness, he comments on the changeableness of Orsino's disposition (72–7). This comment comes just after his song, which has been chosen by Orsino for its supposedly simple naturalness ('It is old and plain . . . And dallies with the innocence of love/Like the old age', 43–8). Though it is in fact a highly artificial dirge for a lover who has been 'slain by a fair cruel maid'. All the apparatus of 'sad cypress', 'yew', 'black coffin', an obscure grave and 'A thousand sighs' is manipulated to achieve the maximum effect of sentimental solemnity. Feste appreciates the moodiness of Orsino and uses his professional skill to provide whatever his 'melancholy' paymaster wants.

However, there is more depth and intensity to the treatment of love than this. The chief focus of interest in this scene is the delicacy of Viola's situation. She is a woman who is actually in love with Orsino, and what comes across is the long-suffering nature of her devotion in her seemingly hopeless plight. Her dialogue with Orsino is a virtual confession of love which only the audience understands (though points are registered which will subsequently come back into Orsino's mind with fresh significance). Thus, to Orsino's question, 'thine eye/Hath stayed upon some favour that it loves. Hath it not, boy?' she replies, 'A little, by your favour' (23–5); and she agrees with poignant emphasis to his statement that men's loves are 'more giddy and infirm' than women's (33–5). The climax comes with her piercingly beautiful speech about 'Patience on a monument'

(110–18) – where 'Patience' means not merely 'quietly waiting' but 'suffering' (from Latin *patio* = 'I suffer, endure'). Viola/Cesario uses the circumlocution, 'My father had a daughter loved a man', to suggest that the reference is to 'his' sister, but gets much closer to the true situation by adding, 'As it might be, perhaps, were I a woman/I should your lordship'. The mask is all but dropped when Orsino asks if this sister died of her unrequited love, and Viola replies:

> I am all the daughters of my father's house
> And all the brothers too; and yet I know not. (119–120)

Indeed, Viola has to change the subject very rapidly – which she does with her immediately following question, 'Sir, shall I to this lady?' She gets away with taking such a risk because of Orsino's obsession with Olivia; but the emotional temperature has been raised to the point where the audience feels that she has all but made a declaration of love – and in a context that reveals her love to be the vibrantly real thing, as opposed to the conventional love-melancholy of Orsino and the studied exaggeration of Feste's song.

Act II, Scene v

The duping of Malvolio begins. Sir Toby, Sir Andrew and Fabian watch in hiding as Malvolio picks up a letter, dropped in his path by Maria, in which Olivia seems to urge him to put on an air of authority, to wear yellow stockings and have his legs cross-gartered, and to smile.

The introduction of Fabian as one of the three eavesdroppers on Malvolio is unexpected. It may be that Shakespeare originally intended Feste to be of the party, but substituted a new character, Fabian, on finding that Feste had acquired too heavy a part.

The gulling of Malvolio is a comic masterpiece, made to seem plausible (though reflection would suggest that Malvolio would in reality probably need more persuasive evidence than this) by his predisposition to think very highly of himself. Even before he picks up the letter he is strongly inclined to believe that Olivia is infatuated with him; and perhaps Maria has been working on him with a few hints, as suggested by his remark that 'Maria once told me she [Olivia] did affect me' (24–5). He indulges in compensatory fantasies in which he imagines himself in such favour with Olivia that he is able to work off old scores against his enemies, especially Sir Toby, and when he finds the letter he is already in the frame of mind to construe it as encouragement from Olivia to treat her as a loving equal and 'Be opposite [= contrary, aggressive] with a kinsman, surly with servants' (150–1).

Malvolio's attitude and language are also made to contrast with those of his hidden watchers, whose words, as well as his, are heard by the audience in a comic antiphony of pomposity and bathos, as when Malvolio imagines himself summoning Sir Toby with the words: 'I extend my hand to him thus, quenching my familiar smile with an austere regard of control . . . ', and Sir Toby cuts in with the aside: 'And does not Toby take you a blow o' the lips then?' (67–70). The impatience of Sir Toby – who has to be restrained several times by Fabian – further contributes to the comic tension, since it threatens to give away the presence of the eavesdroppers to Malvolio; and in most performances of this scene there is much scuttling about on stage as Sir Toby and the others peer out from their hiding places and hastily withdraw again, as Malvolio turns in their direction, to prevent themselves being seen. There may even be stage-directions built into the text to this effect: Honigmann, for example, suggests that when Malvolio reaches the word 'revolve' in the fake letter (145) a pun is, as it were, acted out, since 'revolve' means both 'consider' and 'turn', and on reading it aloud Malvolio makes a turn which almost reveals the eavesdroppers to him (see Macmillan text, p. 94). A further level of farce is added by Sir Andrew, whose stupidity makes him unable to grasp what is obvious enough to his companions – and, of course, to the audience as well. Thus the bawdy implications in Malvolio's comment, 'These be her very C's, her U's and her T's ['cut' = the female organ]; and thus makes she her great P's', are made to stand out all the more coarsely as a result of Sir Andrew's puzzled question, 'Her C's, her U's and her T's? Why that?' (89–92).

Finally, Maria makes a brief reappearance at the end of the scene to find out whether her trick has worked, and by letting the audience know that the yellow stockings and cross-gartering which Malvolio has decided to adopt with such alacrity are things that Olivia detests she whets the audience's appetite for further developments. We cannot wait to see what the next encounter between mistress and steward will be like.

Act III, Scene i

Viola encounters Feste, and then, more briefly, Sir Toby and Sir Andrew, as she is on her way with another message to Olivia. She is given a private interview with Olivia, who admits the deception practised with the ring and confesses her love for 'Cesario'.

The opening dialogue between Viola and Feste is typical of the verbal fencing that often goes on between the witty characters in Shakespearian comedy. It focuses on the question of fools and foolery, and serves to remind the audience that folly, in this play, is not the monopoly of the Fool but is – notwithstanding the importance of social position in this hierarchical world – something of a leveller. As Feste puts it, 'Foolery, sir, does walk about the orb like the sun, it shines everywhere. I would be sorry, sir, but the fool should be as oft with your master as with my mistress' (40–3). Feste himself is no ordinary fool; he is superior in intelligence to most of the people around him. But his economic dependence is also apparent in this scene – for example, Viola gives Feste some money, and Feste, who has to earn his living by such tricks, doubles the amount by cleverly begging another coin. Left alone, Viola reflects that such a fool is a wise fool (in a speech which is generally agreed to be a tribute to the cleverness of Robert Armin, the actor who belonged to the same company as Shakespeare and probably took the part of Feste). By contrast, the stupid, rather than wise fool is exemplified in Sir Andrew, who shows his callowness by wondering at the rarity of Viola's courtly language when addressing Olivia (87–94).

However, the most important part of the scene is to be found in the private dialogue between Viola/Cesario and Olivia. Here Olivia breaks through the conventional barriers of social behaviour so important in the Elizabethan period, and discards the reticence expected of women (thus flouting the sexual code of the time as well) to make a frank avowal of her love for Cesario. It is possible, as some editors suggest, that she believes the 'boy' to be a young nobleman in disguise, though the riddling nature of the words they exchange at lines 141–8 makes it difficult to be sure what is in their respective minds. When Olivia asks Cesario what 'he' thinks of her, 'he' replies, 'That you do think you are not what you are' – which may mean either that Olivia forgets herself, or that she imagines herself to be in love with Cesario. Olivia's response to this – 'If I think so, I think the same of you', is equally ambiguous: her 'If' casts doubt on whether Olivia agrees with what Cesario has said, but she probably means, 'I think *you* forget yourself'. But the words also suggest doubt of Cesario's identity, even though Olivia herself must be unaware of the justification for such doubt. Cesario then retorts: 'Then think you right; I am not what I am', as if confirming what Olivia has said; but what she is actually confirming (i.e. that she is in reality a woman) is only appreciated by the audience. Finally, Olivia's 'I would you were as I would have you be' (i.e. 'my lover') produces from Viola a further ambiguous question – 'Would it be better, madam, than I am?' Again, the audience knows that this would create an impossible situation, while Olivia is simply tantalised by the prospect of a 'better' state of affairs in which Cesario would have dropped 'his' mask and become the suitor that Olivia would like 'him' to be. This brief exchange is thus bafflingly ironic, but absorbingly so for the spectators, who can find several possibilities of meaning in it at the same time.

Despite all this teasing ambiguity the outcome for both speakers is a passionate declaration of feeling. Olivia swears by the highest standards of purity and integrity ('By maidhood, honour, truth') that she loves Cesario, and Cesario takes a comparable oath ('by innocence' and 'youth') that 'he' has 'One heart, one bosom, and one truth' which are dedicated to no woman. But what Olivia takes for a denial is understood by the audience as affirmation of Viola's love for Orsino, and what Olivia intends as assertion of love for Cesario is understood by the audience to be an illusion. Each one is tangled in confusingly ambiguous words, and yet each is honest and forthright in what she says.

Act III, Scene ii

Sir Andrew is again ready to leave, as he is still making no progress with Olivia, but he is once more persuaded to stay by Sir Toby and Fabian, who tell him that he will impress her if he challenges Cesario to a duel. Sir Toby and Fabian see the possibility of sport in this, and they intend to spur on Cesario. Maria calls them to see Malvolio, yellow-stockinged, cross-gartered and smiling.

In this brief scene a new hoax is contrived by Sir Toby and Fabian which will add more complexity to the comedy, and the audience's appetite is whetted for the encounter to come between Malvolio and Olivia. In view of the passionate frankness with which the latter has just declared her love for Cesario (II.i) it is doubly comic that Sir Andrew should be made to think that fighting Cesario and hurting 'him' 'in eleven places' (34) will win over Olivia; and it is similarly absurd that Malvolio believes his outlandish fashion will please his supposedly doting mistress. The baiting of the two foolish would-be suitors goes ahead.

Act III, Scene iii

Although Antonio's devotion has decided him to follow Sebastian (see II.i), despite the danger to himself as a man who has offended Orsino, he cannot risk exposing himself by joining Sebastian in his tour of the city sights. However, he lends Sebastian his purse and agrees to meet him at their lodging.

This functional scene reminds the audience of the existence of Viola's brother and sets up the business of the purse, which will become important towards the end of the next scene.

Act III, Scene iv

Maria warns Olivia that Malvolio is behaving very strangely. When he enters, dressed, as he thinks, according to Olivia's wishes, and quoting what are to her incomprehensible phrases from her supposed letter, she thinks he is mad, and orders him to be given special attention. He behaves in what he imagines to be appropriately aloof fashion with Sir Toby, Fabian and Maria, who, for their part, treat him as a lunatic who must be humoured. Sir Andrew brings the challenge he has written to Cesario, which is read aloud; but Sir Toby prefers to deliver it by word of mouth and in a fiercer style. Olivia enters with Viola/Cesario, deploring the latter's hardness of heart, and after her exit Sir Toby corners Cesario, terrifying 'him' with an account of Sir Andrew's prowess as a fighter. Sir Toby offers to make peace between them, but in speaking to Sir Andrew deliberately exaggerates Cesario's courage and skill. Sir Andrew backs off, and offers his horse as a bribe to settle the quarrel. Sir Andrew tells Cesario that 'he' will have to make at least a pretence of fighting to save his opponent's oath. At the crucial moment Antonio enters and, mistaking Cesario for Sebastian, takes up the quarrel on the young 'man's' behalf. Sir Toby steps in on behalf of Sir Andrew, and a serious fight is only prevented by the appearance of two of Orsino's officers, who arrest Antonio. Still thinking that Viola/Cesario is Sebastian, Antonio asks for his purse back. Viola is mystified, and Antonio is disgusted by what seems to him rank ingratitude. He is led off prisoner. Viola, however, has caught his use of the name, Sebastian, and has hope that her brother is, after all, alive.

Olivia is reaching a state of extreme agitation as a result of her infatuation with Cesario, which heightens still more the comedy of Malvolio's conviction that she is in love with *him*. He casts all caution to the winds, interprets everything in the light of Olivia's supposed concern for him (e.g. her calling for Sir Toby, at line 67, becomes in

Malvolio's distorted view, 'No worse man than Sir Toby to look to me!', 70–1), and is absolutely certain that the evidence is all in his favour: 'Why, everything adheres together, that no dram of a scruple, no scruple of a scruple, no obstacle, no incredulous or unsafe circumstance – what can be said? – nothing that can be, can come between me and the full prospect of my hopes' (84–9).

It is this egregious self-confidence of Malvolio's which makes his baiting at the hands of Sir Toby, Maria and Fabian receive the audience's wholehearted approval. If he were to entertain a few modest doubts about his capacity to win the love of such a woman as Olivia, we might feel more sympathy for him as the victim of a plot; but we see that he is indeed 'sick of self-love', as Olivia had said at I.v.92, and that the plot against him has merely served to expose what was there in his character all the time. As such, he is a fitting butt of the comedy. To treat him as a madman, however, may seem to be going a bit too far. Yet there is justification for that, too, since Malvolio has shown himself to be excessively lacking in self-critical awareness. The rather cruel extravagance displayed in his tormentors' pretence that he is possessed by a devil is also appropriate to a character like Malvolio who has made such a fetish of his gravity and decorum. Nevertheless, as we have seen before, Shakespeare keeps another dimension in view by reminding us that there is a place for Malvolio when he performs his proper function as a steward and keeps to his proper social position. Olivia 'would not have him miscarry' for half of her dowry.

The parallel duping of Sir Andrew has a similar justification in that his equally egregious folly and lack of self-knowledge in thinking that Olivia would ever stoop to marry such a numbskull as himself, simply asks for ridicule. But here, too, there seems a risk of things going too far when Sir Andrew is egged on to challenge Cesario to a duel which, as Sir Toby knows, the foolish knight has neither the courage nor the skill to maintain. The excuse, of course, is that Sir Toby has enough common sense and understanding of character to realise that the opponent will be equally inept and afraid – and the audience is also aware that Cesario is likely to behave with feminine timidity rather than masculine machismo. The comedy can therefore be enjoyed in relative security. All this, however, is upset when Antonio comes on the scene and mistakes Viola/Cesario for Sebastian. Sir Toby immediately recognises that here is a serious opponent and so he takes over from Sir Andrew. The result is a situation which is no longer comic, but one fraught with real danger, for we are clearly meant to see Sir Toby as an equally serious fighter.

Chance resolves this situation in the form of the officers who arrest

Antonio (though it is chance for which the audience has been prepared by the information already given in III.iii); but by the same token a new element of anxiety and tension is introduced, which is intensified by the 'wickedness' of disguise (see II.ii.27) causing Antonio to mistake Viola for Sebastian. An almost tragic note is sounded as Antonio bitterly denounces the supposed ingratitude of Sebastian (378–83) – though this is deflated somewhat by the First Officer's brusque comment, 'The man grows mad', which allies Antonio's behaviour with the more grotesque 'madness' of Malvolio. But the comedy is again rescued, after the departure of Antonio, by Viola's comment in an aside to the audience which shows that she guesses herself to have been mistaken for her brother. The effect of this is to reassure us that true identities will eventually be restored; and her hopes for her brother's life point towards the likelihood of an ultimately happy, rather than unhappy, ending. Indeed, her paradoxical exclamation, 'O, if it prove [i.e. 'if this really proves to be the case'],/Tempests are kind, and salt waves fresh in love' (397–8), suggests a conversion of the traditionally tragic symbol of storm into happiness, and of the bitterness of the sea, with its suggestion of uncertainty and instability, into the sweetness of love.

The final remarks from Sir Toby, Fabian and Sir Andrew indicate a new development in the 'quarrel' between the two reluctant duellists, as Sir Andrew, growing bold again now that he thinks Viola/Cesario is more cowardly than himself, exclaims, 'I'll after him again and beat him'. Is a third crisis about to occur? Not if it involves any real display of valour on Sir Andrew's part. As Sir Toby says (and in conclusion to the whole scene) 'I dare lay any money, 'twill be nothing yet'.

Act IV, Scene i

Feste, sent by Olivia to bid Viola/Cesario come to her, mistakes Sebastian for Cesario, and is rebuffed. Sir Andrew enters, with Sir Toby and Fabian; he also mistakes Sebastian for Cesario, strikes him, and is beaten for his pains. Sir Toby intervenes, Feste goes off to tell Olivia, and the latter arrives just as Sir Toby is engaging Sebastian in fight. She orders Sir Toby to leave, apologises to Sebastian, whom she likewise takes for Cesario, and Sebastian, dazed and bewildered, accepts Olivia's invitation to enter her house.

This is a scene of confusing action, to which mistaken identity is the key. Feste, Sir Andrew, Sir Toby and Olivia all in turn mistake Sebastian for his sister, and therefore behave in ways that utterly bewilder him. His acceptance of Olivia's invitation, though it puzzles him, hints at love at first sight. Thus comedy, farce, danger and, finally, romance are all extracted from the situation in rapid succession. There is again a transition from prose to verse, with Olivia's entrance at line 45.

Act IV, Scene ii

Feste, disguised as a priest, Sir Topas, pretends to visit Malvolio who is now imprisoned as a madman. Then he pretends to visit him in his own character as the Fool, and in different voices simulates a dialogue between himself as Sir Topas and himself as Feste, in which the latter is rebuked for speaking to Malvolio. During this second phase of impersonation Malvolio begs Feste to fetch him writing materials so that he can inform Olivia of the way he is being abused.

This scene is in prose, except for the snatches of song which Feste sings. It gives a further twist to the theme of disguise and false, or falsified, identity in that Feste takes on the appearance of Sir Topas, even speaking a dialogue between his two personae of priest and Fool, and Malvolio is treated as a madman possessed by a devil. The 'mad' world into which Sebastian believes he has just stepped in IV.i is parodied in the farcical distortions of this scene so that the two scenes almost blend into one piece of crazy, continuous action. Feste, the Fool, provides a common thread with his play upon the idea of folly. Compare, for example, the way he takes up Sebastian's phrase, 'vent thy folly', in IV.i.10–14, and, in the present scene, the way that he answers Malvolio's 'I am as well in my wits, fool, as thou art' with the retort, 'But as well? Then you are mad indeed, if you be no better in your wits than a fool' (91–3). Furthermore, there seems to be a deliberate echo of his words to Sebastian, 'Nothing that is so, is so' (spoken when Sebastian was mistaken for Cesario, IV.i.9) in the nonsense speech which he makes when disguised as Sir Topas: 'for as the old hermit of Prague that never saw pen and ink very wittily said to a niece of King Gorboduc: that that is, is. So I, being Master Parson, am Master Parson; for what is "that" but "that"? And "is" but "is"?' (IV.ii.12–16).

Behind such questions lie serious philosophical problems about the nature of being, and yet at the same time they are merely gibberish invented by Feste for the spurious character of Sir Topas. As far as the audience is concerned, however, so much highly farcical action is going on that it scarcely has time to consider the intellectual implications of these words; but what it is aware of – and these words serve to enhance such consciousness – is the way all simple appearances are at odds. Viola is not what she seems to be; Sebastian is not what he is taken for, nor Malvolio either; and Feste, it seems, is whatever persona it suits him to adopt. Moreover, as so frequently in Shakespeare, the audience retains a kind of peripheral awareness that all the characters are, in any case, simply playing parts – i.e. that they are actors in a comedy which is itself all make-believe.

Act IV, Scene iii

Sebastian muses on the strangeness of his situation. Olivia enters and urges him to plight his troth to her in the presence of the priest she brings with her. He agrees.

This scene is continuous with the 'madness' of the previous scenes. Sebastian's bewilderment is expressed in a soliloquy which shows him poised on the point of indecision as to whether he should regard himself or Olivia as mad, and yet seeming to find a reasonableness and orderliness in what he is experiencing. He even has an eye to the main chance as well, as he seems happy to accept the 'flood of fortune' (11) which has so inexplicably come his way – though there is nothing dishonest in what he does, and, as far as we can tell, his intentions in accepting Olivia's astonishing kindness to him are honourable, for, having agreed to the betrothal, he declares that 'having sworn truth' he 'ever will be true' (33). If Malvolio has been led into a world of preposterous illusion by the fake letter which spoke of some having 'greatness thrust upon 'em' (II.v.147), Sebastian's new greatness seems to be just as fantastic, but part of the real world. Unlike Malvolio, however, he does express some healthy scepticism about what is happening to him (e.g. 'there's something in't/That is deceivable [= deceptive]', 20–1), and he is not so egregiously complacent. There is also both a parallel and a contrast to be drawn between 'Sir Topas' in the preceding scene and the figure of the priest in this one. Both are introduced in aid of an illusion, but 'Sir Topas' is an entirely spurious priest, whereas the present one is a 'holy man' (23) and a 'good man' (32), before whom both Olivia and Sebastian intend to swear the most serious of oaths. Nevertheless, the sense of 'madness' is still sustained, for Olivia continues to think in terms of the false 'Cesario'; and Sebastian, on his own admission, is caught in a state of bewildered uncertainty between reason, madness and 'faith'.

Act V, Scene i

After a preliminary display of his wit Feste goes as a messenger to bring Olivia to Orsino. Antonio, under arrest, is brought before the

Duke, where he is accused of having attacked certain Illyrian ships. Viola/Cesario intercedes for him because he drew his sword on her side, but Antonio complains that it was for this 'ungrateful boy' that he exposed himself to danger in Orsino's territory and that he lent 'him' his purse, which is now being denied. As Olivia enters his case is put aside. She is adamant in rejecting Orsino's love-suit, and he begins to suspect that the reason she does so is that Cesario has stolen her love. In his jealousy he threatens to do Cesario harm; Viola/ Cesario submits to Orsino, but Olivia urges 'him', as virtually her 'husband', to resist, and when 'he' denies any relationship between them she brings in the priest who, she declares, has witnessed their betrothal. At this point Sir Andrew enters complaining of the hurt done to him and Sir Toby by Cesario – who, of course, denies it. Sir Toby enters asking for the surgeon whom Feste is supposed to have been fetching. Olivia orders the two wounded men to be looked after; then Sebastian appears, with an apology for having hurt her kinsman. The presence of the brother and sister together leads to the revelation of their true identities and to their joyful reunion. Orsino now realises that his 'boy', Cesario, is actually a woman who loves him, and he accepts her as his wife. Olivia proposes that the double wedding – hers to Sebastian and Viola's to Orsino, shall take place at her house. Feste brings in Malvolio's letter protesting against his ill-usage, and with Malvolio's own appearance the plot is exposed. Fabian accepts that he and Sir Toby are to blame, but pleads that it should all be treated as a joke. Malvolio departs in anger, but Orsino sends someone after him to make peace. The play ends with Feste alone on the stage singing the song, 'When that I was and a little tiny boy'.

In this long concluding scene the various plot entanglements are disentangled and the confusions of identity are sorted out. There remain a few loose ends, however. For example, the business of Antonio is not properly wound up. At line 100 Orsino breaks off his interrogation of Antonio with the words, 'But more of that anon. Take him aside'; but it seems that Antonio remains on stage to witness Sebastian's appearance for the first time alongside Viola, for at lines 224–6 he wonders 'Which is Sebastian?' What happens to Antonio thereafter is not clear – we can only presume that Shakespeare intended him to be recognised as Sebastian's benefactor and on that account to be forgiven for his past offences against Orsino. There is also some seemingly incomplete business to do with the Captain who made a brief appearance with Viola in I.ii. He does not reappear in the play, but in this scene Viola refers to his having her 'maiden weeds [garments]' in his keeping (256–8), and a little later explains that he is held in prison at Malvolio's suit (276–9). Olivia thereupon says that Malvolio must free him, but we hear no more of the captain. As Honigmann notes, there also seems to be some inconsistency between II.i.18–19, where Sebastian explains to Antonio that he has lost a sister who was born in the same hour as himself, and the present reunion of Sebastian and Viola, where part of the evidence of identification consists in Viola's remembering the fact that her father died on her thirteenth birthday. This could, of course, mean that both she and Sebastian were 13 on that day, but, if so, it is odd that she does not refer to their being twins.

However, not too much importance should be attached to such flaws. They are probably the result of the play's having been written at great speed (and in the white heat of inspiration); and in any case they would scarcely be noticed in the hurry-scurry of theatrical performance. The main points are clearly enough established, and the audience is likely to be much more interested in seeing how the problems caused by Viola's disguise and her physical similarity to Sebastian are sorted out. The absorbing business of this scene is tension and its resolution: the crossed-love relationships of Orsino, Olivia and Cesario are straightened out; the conventional happy ending, with appropriate marriages, which is expected of romantic comedy, is brought about; the trick played on Malvolio is likewise brought to conclusion, and it is to be presumed that Fabian's plea for forgiveness for all those involved is granted. As he says, it is unfitting that any quarrel or 'brawl' should 'Taint the condition of this present hour' (358–9).

Nevertheless, some painful moments are experienced by various characters. Antonio, for example, speaks of his disillusionment in seeing a young man whom he has so generously befriended turn away from him in rank ingratitude and become as cool towards him as if they had been estranged for twenty years (86–90) – and the fact that the audience knows that this is a misapprehension does not lessen the painfulness of the experience as far as Antonio is concerned. Orsino has shown himself so much in the grip of 'a savage jealousy' that, despite his fondness for Viola/Cesario – perhaps, indeed, the more enraged by his affection for the boy now that he thinks 'him' a rival – he is ready to 'sacrifice the lamb' that he loves (119–31); and, for her part, Viola has to hear herself cruelly insulted by the man she loves, while patiently accepting the anger and threats of death that come from him. Olivia, too, suffers the extreme anguish of seeing, to all intents and purposes, the very man who has just vowed everlasting love as her betrothed husband, not only deny her, but willingly abandon her for the sake of a master whom 'he' declares that 'he' loves:

> More than I love these eyes, more than my life,
> More by all mores than ere I shall love wife (135–6).

Less seriously, Sir Andrew and Sir Toby receive 'bloody coxcombs' and along with Feste and Fabian they get themselves into deep disgrace with Olivia. We hear, too, of misfortune suffered by the Captain who helped Viola at the beginning of the play – an echo, perhaps, of the unmerited misfortune which befalls Antonio after helping her brother, Sebastian.

As we have seen, all these anxieties and causes of distress are remedied (or we can reasonably assume that they are) once the true situation is made known. But can the same be said of the indignities and afflictions imposed on Malvolio? His letter to Olivia shows him to be, as he says himself, 'the madly-used Malvolio' (312); but Orsino's laconic comment, 'This savours not much of distraction' (315), endorses what the audience feels to be the justice and truth of his complaint. This is further emphasised by Malvolio's actual appearance on stage and the speech he delivers at lines 332–46, which vividly communicates his side of the case. It is one thing for Sir Toby and his friends to make fun of an egregious egotist to the extent of treating him as a madman (behaviour which an Elizabethan audience would probably be more ready than a modern one to accept), but it is quite another thing to be the unwilling victim of such treatment. This powerfully compelling speech of Malvolio's makes us feel what it is like from his point of view. Previously, while the plot was being acted out, we might well have laughed at it as merely uproarious farce, but that simple reaction becomes more complicated now. Fabian explains, and Olivia sympathises; which no doubt mitigates the sense of injustice – though Feste still harps on the theme of revenge (372–9). Malvolio, however, remains unappeased, and the last words we hear from him are: 'I'll be revenged on the whole pack of you!' (380). The effect of this exit is softened a little by Orsino's 'Pursue him and entreat him to a peace' (382), but not completely expunged. The memory of Malvolio's resentment lingers on.

Finally, Feste's closing song, with its haunting refrain, 'With hey, ho, the wind and the rain', allows the storm theme of tragedy to disturb the would-be reconciling notes of comedy. Its concluding words, 'And we'll strive to please you every day', underline the make-believe nature of the play, and they also remind us that its purpose is to entertain. By so doing they help to soften the sardonic and satirical burden of the song. But as an epilogue to the play it is curiously less cheerful than might be expected. The appropriately festive subjects of drinking and merry-making are celebrated within it, but they are transposed, via such lines as 'By swaggering could I never thrive' and 'With tosspots still had drunken heads', into a somewhat melancholy minor key; and the reiteration of 'For the rain it raineth every day' seems to insist on a pessimistic view not only of the weather, but of life itself. The traditionally happy ending is thus muted, and the audience is sent away from the theatre in a more complex, and more thoughtful, mood than is usually associated with comedy.

3 THEMES AND ISSUES

3.1 LOVE AND ROMANCE

The play begins, 'If music be the food of love, play on'. The music which is played is of a languishing, heart-rending kind, and it would seem that Orsino listens to it with rapt attention – until, that is, it palls, and, in his changeable way, he orders it to cease. Thus *Twelfth Night* opens drenched in sentiment; and sentiment focused on that most sentimental of topics, love. Virtually all Shakespeare's comedies are on this theme, unlike those, for example, of Ben Jonson, which are concerned with such things as confidence tricks, petty crime, vicious self-indulgence and contemptible follies – coarse, unsentimental, hard-nosed themes. Yet to dub Shakespeare the tenderminded, and Jonson the tough-minded, comic writers of the Elizabethan period would be to do Shakespeare at least a grave disservice. No one can evoke the vibrant, emotional world of love, as this opening illustrates, more movingly than Shakespeare, but he also shows a complex awareness, not only of other dimensions of comedy, but of the multilayered and kaleidoscopically varied nature of the love-experience. For him it is both an old-fashioned and a very modern subject, which can both pluck the heart-strings and make us split our sides with laughter.

The love he presents on stage is romantic love: that is to say, it is love as shown in 'romance' stories – those tales of handsome, heroic young men and beautiful, pure young women who love one another but also endure crosses and frustrations in love (for, as Shakespeare says in *A Midsummer Night's Dream*, 'The course of true love never did run smooth'), and who inhabit a primary-coloured world of make-believe which is more exotic, more thrilling, more full of magical possibilities and wonderful reverberations than the world of everyday business and domestic life can ever be. This world of romance is also one where men and women feel more intensely and deeply than ordinary people do, and as such it satisfies – as the ordinary, familiar, commonplace world cannot – the profoundly human need for passionate experience centred upon such ideals as selflessness, loyalty, patience and dedication to the well-being of a beloved person.

Because it is so idealistic and so extravagantly larger-than-life romance is also, of course, highly vulnerable; and romance therefore readily invites the anti-romantic. Indeed, if it is not too much of a paradox, it may be said that romance depends for its viability on the anti-romantic: so much does it seem to transcend, and deny, the flaws and limitations of the prosaically real world that it is only by incorporating a criticism of its extravagances within its presentation that the emotional validity of romance can be protected from the corrosive effects of exposure to the real world. On roughly the same principle as a Roman general enjoying a triumphal procession in honour of his victories would be accompanied by a slave who constantly reminded him of his ordinary, human fallibility, so the characters in romantic love comedy need to be accompanied by others who are more down-to-earth and sceptical, if not downright cynical. Such thesis and anti-thesis is certainly of the essence in Shakespearian comedy, which, though it is called 'romantic comedy', is really a sophisticated blend of romantic and anti-romantic attitudes, calculated to get the best out of both the ideal and the real worlds.

To return, therefore, to Orsino: in his opening speech love is treated as something emotional, evocative and expansive (its 'capacity/Receiveth as the sea'), but it is also seen as counter-productive since whatever enters there 'falls into abatement and low price'. Its very dependence on the imagination, which enables it to be so richly fascinating, also makes it capable of deteriorating into something absurd and irrational; it is 'high fantastical' in both positive and negative ways.

In these lines Orsino may well speak more wisely than he is aware of. His own conscious attitude is that of the 'despised lover', well known in the romantic tradition, who devotes his love and service to 'a fair, cruel maid' (see Feste's song, II.iv.53) who cannot, or will not, return his love. He has lost his heart to Olivia, or – in a more romantic figure so common as to have become a cliché – his heart (the seat of the emotions) has migrated from his own body to take up residence in that of his beloved. This is the meaning behind the pun on hunting the 'hart' in his exchange with Curio:

CURIO	Will you go hunt, my lord?
ORSINO	What, Curio?
CURIO	The hart.
ORSINO	Why, so I do, the noblest that I have. (I.i.16–19)

The pun may excite a good-natured groan from the audience; but, if so, that is not inappropriate. The double meaning represents both the romantic provenance of Orsino's attitude and the ridiculous nature of the convention which it has become. And this ambiguity of response is reinforced by many details elsewhere in the play – not least by Feste's comment (which comes in II.iv, immediately after another piece of powerfully emotive love-music) that Orsino is a man whose 'mind is a very opal', i.e. he changes the colours of his mood from one moment to the next as the whim of sentiment leads him.

The play has many other examples of love which is similarly ambiguous in value. For instance, Olivia's devotion to the memory of her dead brother is seen by Orsino as an indication of how whole-heartedly she will give herself when she does fall in love (I.i.33–9), but Sir Toby treats her grief lightly: 'What a plague means my niece to take the death of her brother thus? I am sure care's an enemy to life' (I.iii.1–3). The fact that Olivia is so quickly drawn to Viola/ Cesario (and that she so easily switches her love to Sebastian once the false identities have been sorted out) likewise casts doubt on the depth of her grief: the seven years' cloistering to which she has vowed herself then looks as much an affectation as Orsino's moody passion. On the other hand, the hints we are given that Feste has a mistress (see Honigmann, p. 12) suggest that, for all his carefully cultivated worldly wisdom, he, too, is not immune from the folly of love. Nor, it seems, is Sir Toby, though his falling in love (if that is the right phrase for it) with Maria has more to do with her clever wit and strength of personality than with sentiment. Likewise Sir Andrew's and Malvolio's pursuit of Olivia has little to do with romance and everything to do with self-interest (and deplorable lack of self-knowledge). In Malvolio's case it is almost a corrupt variation of love in which egotism displaces concern for the beloved. As Olivia correctly diagnoses (though, at the time she is referring to his haughty treatment of Feste, and not to any avowal of affection), Malvolio is 'sick of self-love' and tastes 'with a distempered [diseased] appetite' (I.v.92–3).

Even within the tradition of romance falling in love is often represented as an experience which is tantamount to being struck down by a disease. The bright young man or woman is transformed into a pale, languishing creature at death's door, as in the song, 'Come away, come away, death' (II.iv.50–64). Orsino is yet again an illustration of this: his opening words represent music as 'the food of love' leading to 'surfeiting' and consequent sickening; and though he speaks of Olivia as having a health-giving power ('Methought she purged the air of pestilence', 20), 'pestilence', meaning 'plague', again associates love with the idea of sickness. The same image is used by Olivia herself, when feeling her desires aroused by Viola/ Cesario, she asks herself, 'Even so quickly may one catch the plague?' (I.v.298). And, above all, in defending the depth and sincerity of woman's love against Orsino's unreasonable assertion that the female heart is too small to hold a passion like his (II.iv.93–6), Cesario speaks of 'his' supposed sister's unrequited love as a canker which secretly undermined her health, till:

> She pined in thought,
> And with a green and yellow melancholy
> She sat like Patience on a monument
> Smiling at grief.

There is little doubt that this reference to a 'sister's' love is Viola's oblique way of alluding to her own love for Orsino; it is certainly understood as such by the audience, if not by the Duke himself. Viola is thus to be counted as one more of the characters in the play who are afflicted by some version or other of love-sickness. Yet she fully commands the audience's sympathy. Sickness in her case is combined with a practical energy and vigour, displayed in her 'Cesario' role, which counterbalances the enervating effect of passive submission to the romantic disease. Her love may be a painful affliction, but she exerts herself and finds a way to serve her beloved in a positive fashion. In this respect it may be compared with Antonio's love for Sebastian. This is a non-erotic form of love arising solely from Antonio's response to the virtues and personal qualities of Sebastian – unless, that is, one insists on regarding it as homosexual (for which there is little justification in the text). Like Viola, he translates his love into generous, selfless action; and, like her, he has to endure the bitterness of seeing the man he admires turn, apparently, into something of a moral monster. The main difference is that his love seems exempt from the taint of disease. Antonio may be the only character in the play to love in a totally disinterested manner.

3.2 TIME

As we have seen, Viola has to suffer the pangs of romantic love-sickness, but also manages to act constructively. Yet there are limits to her powers of action. She herself recognises this when she contrives her disguise as Cesario and gets her obliging Captain to present her at Orsino's court: this is as much as she can do, the rest, she says, must be left to time ('What else may hap to time I will commit,/Only shape thou thy silence to my wit', I.ii.58–9). Similarly, although she exerts herself as Orsino's messenger to Olivia and speaks most eloquently on his behalf, the effect of her eloquence (and her person) is to make Olivia fall in love with her false Cesario image, and to bring about complications which are beyond her power to resolve. Again, she feels, 'O time, thou must untangle this, not I!/It is too hard a knot for me t'untie' (II.ii.40–1).

Considered in isolation these comments might suggest a fatalistic attitude to life. But fatalism is appropriate neither to Viola as a character, nor to *Twelfth Night* as a play. There is no sense of weary resignation to unavoidable circumstances; all is too lively, vigorous and active for that. But there is an implicit recognition of the circumscribing limits within which human action can take place and an acceptance of the conditioning effect of time.

In time all things in life grow, change, come to fruition and decay. This is a basic fact to which everyone must accommodate – not least, those young women of marriageable age with whom romantic love comedy is especially concerned. As Orsino reminds Cesario, when urging 'him' to choose a woman younger than himself: 'For women are as roses whose fair flower,/Being once displayed, doth fall that very hour'. Viola/Cesario being in reality 'she', and not 'he' appreciates the truth of this comment more fully than Orsino is aware, and endorses it feelingly: 'And so they are. Alas, that they are so,/To die, even when they to perfection grow' (II.iv.38–41). The implication here is that time is a ceaseless double process of maturation and decay, with life and death treading upon each other's heels – and that women are the ones who feel this paradox most poignantly.

The same theme is echoed in the dialogue between Viola/Cesario and Olivia at III.i, when Olivia virtually makes love to the seeming youth. She is interrupted by the striking of a clock, which causes her to exclaim:

The clock upbraids me with the waste of time.
Be not afraid good youth; I will not have you.

> And yet, when wit and youth is come to harvest,
> Your wife is like to reap a proper man. (134–7)

The significance of this is complex. Olivia pretends to be overcoming her infatuation and dismissing the youth, as if recognising that her behaviour is a 'waste of time' since it is inappropriate to both her age and situation. The audience, however, is fully aware that she is bluffing, and yet it recognises the very real inappropriateness of her behaviour in view of the true identity of Viola. Over and beyond that, there is further irony in Olivia's reference to Cesario's youthfulness, which promises, to her eyes, a ripe manhood that has not yet come to harvest. As the woman she is in reality Viola stands much nearer to the brink of 'harvest' than Olivia appreciates, but, as the audience knows, that harvest is frustrated by the tantalising situation in which she finds herself. She cannot reap *her* proper man precisely because of the situation which makes her appear an immature youth instead of a mature, marriageable woman. Her time is therefore perilously at risk of being wasted and her 'perfection' of being turned into decay.

A further possible level of meaning can be detected in Olivia's words. She may also be regarded as wasting her time by inappropriately protracted mourning for her dead brother, when the business of a woman in her prime, as she is, is with living, loving and procreation. This point is graphically, and once again ironically, demonstrated by her present attraction to Cesario, which is (though unknown to her) sexually perverse and necessarily barren. The striking of the clock upbraids her and challenges her to use her time appropriately; and this – in a sense – she tries to do by substituting love of the living for love of the dead. But until time makes possible the substitution of Sebastian for Cesario she is trapped in the present time's frustrating situation.

The theme of time makes itself felt in the more farcical areas of the play as well. For example, when Malvolio rebukes Sir Toby and Sir Andrew for their drunken behaviour, he demands, 'Is there no respect of place, persons, nor time in you?' And the reply he receives from Sir Toby is: 'We did keep time, sir, in our catches' (II.iii.95–7). Malvolio likewise anticipates Olivia's self-rebuke in III.i (mentioned above) when in II.v he tells Sir Toby, 'you waste the treasure of your time with a foolish knight' (79–80); and Fabian speaks of time wasted when he mockingly rebukes Sir Andrew for missing his chance with Olivia by not showing sufficient boldness in his treatment of Cesario: 'The double gilt of this opportunity you let wash off, and you are now sailed into the north of my lady's opinion . . . ' (III.ii.25–7). Such references to time are trivial compared with those made by Viola and

Olivia, but they serve to suggest the universality of the theme; and they also remind us that beneath the surface of the rumbustious farce there is a more serious point being made about the unsuitability of both Sir Andrew's and Sir Toby's behaviour to their social rank and time of life. As for Malvolio himself, he, too, is gulled into behaviour which is inappropriate and mistimed. The regularity of time is a metaphor for order, and his presumptuous behaviour is a breach of decorum that smacks of more than personal vanity. Retribution likewise comes from time, as Feste triumphantly announces when he reveals that it was he who played the part of Sir Topas: 'And thus the whirligig of time brings in his revenges' (V.i.379).

By contrast, the role-playing Fool is one who does know the value of time. His satirical wit is directed against failure to observe the requirements of time, and at least two of his songs harp on the passage of time. 'O mistress mine!' dwells on the transience of youth and love, insisting that: 'Present mirth hath present laughter,/What's to come is still unsure' (II.iii.48–9), while 'When that I was and a little tiny boy' sardonically glosses the change from boyhood to 'man's estate', rounding off with a perspective on time itself: 'A great while ago the world began' (V.i.391–410). The very title of the play, *Twelfth Night*, signifies a time – the last of the twelve days of the Christmas festivity – which is given over to merry-making and a sanctioned spell of disorderliness under the Lord of Misrule (a court official appointed to preside over the revels of the season) and in which fools are licensed to vent their folly. Hence Feste, *the* Fool, may be said to occupy a privileged position, not only in Olivia's household, but in the play itself. As an entertainment this, too, has its appropriate timing, and Feste is the one who brings it to its end:

> But that's all one, our play is done,
> And we'll strive to please you every day. (V.i.409–10)

Time is up; the play is finished. The audience has been here to pass the time amusingly, but it has also been kept aware of the passage of time. And if the dilemmas and painful situations into which time puts the characters are what constitute that entertainment, so also is the sense that time will resolve problems and ultimately put things right. The play is, after all, only a play and the audience knows that the guiding hand of the playwright is there timing and keeping control of events. Time in this sense is the forward movement of the action of the play which unfolds the plot, surprising the audience with the delightfully unexpected, but also reassuring with a sense of developing, structured time – a fashioned beginning, middle and end. The audience is intuitively aware that in time Viola's disguise will be revealed, that in time she and her brother will meet, and that in time the deception practised on Malvolio will come to light.

Time is thus both tormentor and healer, and it is present under both its aspects in *Twelfth Night*. That its positive rather than negative power will ultimately be shown as the stronger is assured by the fundamentally comic spirit of the play, but the triumph is not a simple one. The forces are delicately poised, and what we see time working out is a subtly variegated comedy.

3.3 THE COMPLEXITY OF SHAKESPEARIAN COMEDY

In its simplest definition a comedy is a play which ends happily, as a tragedy is one which ends unhappily. *Twelfth Night* conforms with this definition in that the lovers are paired off at the end, Viola and Sebastian are reunited and a 'golden time' (V.i.384) is expected. Several of the characters pass through a stressful period before this is achieved, but that in itself is no detraction from comic harmony. The taste of anguish makes the enjoyment of resolution and reunion all the keener; and it will be observed that all Shakespeare's comedies in varying degrees use such paradoxical bitter-sweetness to heighten the joy which their characters feel when the happy ending is finally reached.

However, the tradition of much Greek and Latin comedy (the tradition to which Ben Jonson and the great French writer of comedy, Molière, belong) is satirical and corrective rather than hedonistic. Its aim is to use ridicule as a weapon for exposing fools and rogues, and even more vicious characters, to the scorn of the audience. Laughter is excited, but it is laughter *at* those who depart from the tacitly agreed norms of social behaviour. Such comedy is self-consciously moral; it aims to improve the standard of human conduct, or support an established code of morals; and though it, too, moves towards a happy ending, the targets of its satire are usually punished with humiliation and disgrace rather than extended forgiveness. *Twelfth Night* also has a share in this tradition of comedy. Malvolio is the clearest example. His vanity and social climbing are made the object of the audience's derision via the letter-plot, which is contrived not merely to dupe him into believing a false version of events, but to work upon his pre-existing tendencies. It is because he already has such an inflated opinion of himself and is so uncharitable to others that he falls into the trap that is laid for him. The audience therefore feels that he deserves what happens to him, and it delights to see him get his come-uppance. Less devastatingly, perhaps, but no less pointedly, Sir Andrew Aguecheek is likewise made the butt of comedy. His very title 'Sir', which proclaims him to be a knight, causes him to be exposed to ridicule, since he is woefully inadequate by the standards of courage and nobility associated with knighthood. That he also thinks of himself – or tries to think of himself – as a witty, fashionable man-about-town (with, of course, the slenderest possible justification) makes him a still greater figure of absurdity. And it is appropriate that he, too, should be egregiously gulled.

Twelfth Night is thus composed of the intertwining of two different kinds of comedy; and, as already indicated, the introduction of the characters and sentiments of romance adds a further strand to the complex thread. The result is a highly sophisticated variety of drama which is uniquely Shakespearian. The satirical, sentimental and romantic all interact and are modified by their interaction. For example, the account given in the above paragraph of Sir Andrew as a false knight and self-deluded fool may well strike many sensitive readers or spectators of the play as crudely oversimplified, and perhaps a complete travesty of his character – though just how crudely inaccurate will probably depend, for spectators, on the assumptions made by director and actors in any particular performance. Sir Andrew is repeatedly fooled by Sir Toby, but there is invariably such innocence in his stupidity, such sublime ignorance of his inability to reach the level to which he aspires, that the sting is drawn from the audience's contempt, and its attitude becomes one of affectionate indulgence. There can even be a covert sense of 'there but for the grace of God go I', for it is a common experience to find oneself eclipsed by people of sharper wit, as Sir Andrew finds himself outshone by Sir Toby and Maria, or to make rather desperate attempts to claim credit for talents one envies, but does not possess, as Sir Andrew does when he claims to 'cut a caper' and have 'the back-trick simply as strong as any man in Illyria' (I.iii.121–4). The fact that these are such slight accomplishments adds to the sense of Sir Andrew's folly, but it does not remove the human element. Similarly, the trivial comment 'I was adored once' (a follow-up to Sir Toby's comment that Maria is 'one that adores me', II.iii.185–7) exposes Sir Andrew to ridicule for pretending that he, too, has been the object of loving admiration, but also arouses at least a touch of sympathy for his futile attempt to impress. This, after all, is a play which dramatises love romance, and though the passage belongs to one of the scenes of gulling comedy it is not, and cannot be, insulated from the rest. Only the faintest shadow perhaps of romantic sentiment falls across Sir Andrew's words, but it is enough to affect the predominantly mocking, satirical light which is shed on them.

Malvolio is also capable of arousing sympathy as well as provoking derisive laughter, if the actor playing the part is so disposed. His final 'I'll be revenged on the whole pack of you!' (V.i.38) can become the expression of a deeply-felt sense of wrong. The earlier baiting of Malvolio (II.v) is entirely proportionate to the overweening egotism and ill-disguised presumption which he has displayed in preceding scenes. But when he is confined in the dark house and treated as a madman (IV.ii) his sufferings do indeed seem to go beyond what is justified by his behaviour; though one has to bear in mind that the Elizabethan attitude to madness allowed it to be treated more farcically than now seems proper. Moreover, his protest in the last Act that he has been deluded by 'such clear lights of favour' (V.i.333–46) carries some weight. Obviously, Olivia is not to blame, as she has been no party to the deception, but Malvolio is not to know that. What he is saying, in effect, is that appearances have been created which caused him to think that his behaviour would win approval (and it must be admitted that Olivia does seem to value his gravity and sense of decorum), that he has done his best to fulfil what he believed was expected of him, but that his reward has been disgraceful treatment and humiliation. Retaining a sense of comedy, the audience will judge him wanting in reasonableness and self-knowledge to let himself be carried away so preposterously, but Shakespeare also gives Malvolio such a forcefully expressed point of view that other possibilities are inevitably suggested. And among these is the possibility that Malvolio (in the words of the later tragic play, *King Lear*) 'is more sinned against than sinning'. The audience is therefore compelled to modify its sense of comedy. As Thomas Hardy wrote, three centuries later, 'If you look beneath the surface of any farce you see a tragedy; and, on the contrary, if you blind yourself to the deeper issues of a tragedy you see a farce.' Without going so far as to say that if we look beneath the farcical level of the letter-plot in *Twelfth Night* what we see is the tragedy of Malvolio, it is possible to argue that a degree of sympathy is aroused which breaks down the watertight compartments between 'farce' (or 'comedy') and 'tragedy', and though the play still remains predominantly comic, we are given darker glimpses of maltreatment and abuse which hint at a tragic dimension.

In spite of this, however, *Twelfth Night* does remain a comedy which moves towards the traditionally happy ending. Even at its tensest and most anguished moments the audience still possesses a fundamental awareness that things will come out right. As we have seen, the predicament in which Viola finds herself may be too hard a knot for her to untie, but the audience is granted a god-like perspective by virtue of which it can see what she, from her more limited and confined viewpoint, cannot see. The audience is aware, for example, that Sebastian is alive and therefore knows that her true identity will sooner or later be revealed. And as the play progresses it also has the advantage of knowing that Olivia, in mistaking Sebastian for Cesario, makes a significant step towards transferring her love from a being who can never satisfy her (because that being only *appears* to be a man) to one who is fully qualified to do so. On the more farcical level, the deception of Malvolio is both wonderfully laughable and perceptibly brittle – it treads on the brink of exposure, since the audience knows that the letter must eventually be found to be a forgery. Similarly, the would-be duel between Cesario and Sir Andrew is based on fictitious versions of the contestants' characters which the audience has the immense pleasure of watching Sir Toby create (III.iv); and even though something far more dangerous is threatened when Antonio and Sir Toby take over the duel, the audience is fundamentally reassured by its knowledge that 'Sebastian' is not Sebastian and 'Cesario' is not Cesario. Furthermore, there is a sense that a kind of comic providence is at work, which allows things to go so far and no further – manifested in this instance by the neatness of the stage-direction, 'Enter two OFFICERS', which occurs at the very point when serious bloodshed seems imminent (329). In real life the police cannot be relied on to appear at the convenient moment. In tragedy they appear too late; in comedy they are just in the nick of time. This is a convention which the audience accepts, and it is accepted because it is in harmony with the subtly controlled atmosphere of the play.

The plot, that is to say, is a comic plot; and though the audience is swept along at moments by feelings of high excitement, it never quite loses the sense that what it is watching is a play devised for its entertainment. Again one is reminded of Feste's remark at the very end: 'But that's all one, our play is done,/And we'll strive to please you every day' and in saying this Feste makes himself the spokesman for the comic spirit, daring to remind the audience of the artificiality of the whole performance.

Elsewhere Feste is the spokesman of the comic spirit in a different, but equally important, sense, in that he is the critic of absurdity, explaining the folly of others for the benefit of the audience – and tacitly asking its members to agree with his standard of values. His name, with its suggestion of *fest*ivity, and his role of the

Fool – licensed mocker of sentimentality, irrationality and puritanical narrowness – together mark him out as the antithesis of the
humourless Malvolio. He is supported in this by Sir Toby, who makes
the play's classic statement of the opposition between pleasure and
restraint when he asks Malvolio: 'Dost thou think, because thou art
virtuous, there shall be no more cakes and ale?' (II.iii.117–19). Sir
Toby, however, is a cruder and coarser character than Feste. As his
surname 'Belch' suggests, he expresses his contempt for Malvolio
with a kind of rude noise. Feste's rejection of Malvolio is subtler; it
relies on verbal wit and sharpness of mind. He bewilders the steward
with his role-playing versatility rather than luring him on with false
bait – though both are ways of comically appropriate gulling; and he
represents that supple adaptability which Bergson, the French philo-
sopher of comedy, contrasts with the automaton-like behaviour of
the man who slips on the banana skin.

All forms of stiffness and inflexibility become objects of ridicule to
Feste as impediments to survival. Hence he is enemy not only to
Malvolio's hidebound egotism, but also to the amorous affectation of
Orsino and even the sentimental mourning of his mistress, Olivia –
attitudes which threaten to rigidify into life-denying postures. He
does not in himself represent the perfectly balanced response to all
situations, and he is not always in control of events – as Malvolio
cruelly, but probably with accuracy, points out, 'unless you laugh and
minister occasion to him, he is gagged' (I.v.88–9). But he is a highly
sensitive instrument for selecting the comic inadequacies in others'
responses. He is a means therefore of constantly drawing the
audience's attention to what is absurd and of keeping its critical
intelligence alert. And this, like the consciousness of 'providence'
and of the artificiality of the plot, further contributes to the audience's sense that what it is watching is a comedy. Other attitudes are
allowed their scope – and to such an extent that the divisions
between genres are blurred; but the basic experience remains one of
satisfaction in the resolution of difficulties, laughter at the exposure
of follies, and delight in the nimbleness of man's wit.

3.4 ORDER AND DISORDER

Both Malvolio and Maria rebuke Sir Toby for his disorderly behaviour. For example, in the very first scene in which she appears Maria
tells Sir Toby: 'Ay, but you must confine yourself within the modest
limits of order' (I.iii.8–9); and later in the play Malvolio breaks in on
the roudy carousing of Sir Toby, Sir Andrew and Feste with the

indignant queries: 'Do ye make an ale-house of my lady's house, that ye squeak out your coziers' catches without any mitigation or remorse of voice? Is there no respect of place, persons, nor time in you?' (III.ii.91–5). Malvolio also claims that he has the authority of Olivia to tell Sir Toby that, although she is willing to give him accommodation in her house because he is her kinsman, 'she's nothing allied to your disorders' (100). On the assumption that Olivia is being reported correctly, such comments from three such different persons add up to quite sharp criticism of Sir Toby's conduct. By Elizabethan standards he is in serious breach of decorum and propriety.

Much research during the past fifty years or more has demonstrated how strongly notions of order and 'degree' (or due respect for birth and social rank) were upheld by the Elizabethan establishment. In *Troilus and Cressida* Ulysses's speech to his fellow-warriors attributing the failure of the Greeks in their siege of Troy to dissension within their own army is a representative example of this attitude:

> The specialty of rule hath been neglected
> And look how many Grecian tents do stand
> Hollow upon this plain, so many hollow factions.
> When that the general is not like the hive,
> To whom the foragers shall all repair,
> What honey is expected? Degree being vizarded,
> Th'unworthiest shows as fairly in the mask.
>
> (*Troilus and Cressida*, I.iii.78–84)

The notion was commonplace, and it was convenient politically in that it helped to bolster obedience to a monarchical and aristocratic government; but it was also an integral part of the social and religious thinking of the time. The very structure of the world and of all the creatures who inhabited it was conceived in hierarchial terms, and it was felt that to disturb this intricate pattern of order was to shake the foundations of the universe itself. The riotous behaviour of Sir Toby and his cronies could well therefore attract severe disapproval. He could be seen as a threat to the harmony which comedy proposes as an end for itself, and it could be argued that the wound he receives in his mistaken encounter with Sebastian is a form of retribution brought upon him for flouting order and decorum.

On the other hand, his opposition to Malvolio, as we have seen, reflects a more liberal and 'festive' attitude, peculiarly appropriate to the relaxation of order, hierarchy and discipline for which licence is given in the period of revels from Christmas to Twelfth Night. From this point of view Malvolio may be said to represent order seen in a different light – not as something essential to the well-being of society, but as a repressive and inhibitive force, which also, ironically, encourages egotism by feeding an overweening self-esteem in its instrument, the steward. Or, rather, this is the perversion of order into authoritarianism, which prompts the natural reaction expressed in Sir Toby's disgust. The pendulum of the audience's feeling swings in the opposite direction, till the admittedly disorderly Sir Toby nevertheless seems to represent a more admirable way of life than the pompous Malvolio with his insistence on rules and regulations.

In *Twelfth Night*, however, the principles of order and disorder are not limited to such simplistic opposition. Feste, for example, is also a subverter of order, but one who makes his living by providing services to those who have prestige, power and money in this world, such as singing a song, putting on a professional display of wit, or delivering a message. And both Viola and Sebastian play roles which, if not subversive of order, lead them to breaches of decorum, and to viewing the world, if only for a time, as curiously disorderly, or 'mad'. Her disguise, for example, involves Viola in behaviour unsuited to her sex. She becomes a woman dressed in young man's attire, and she is constrained by her 'Cesario' role to adopt most unwomanly manners when acting as Orsino's proxy wooer of Olivia. She is rebuked for her 'rudeness' by Olivia, and even while defending herself by retorting that her rudeness is of a kind with the way she has been treated ('The rudeness that hath appeared in me have I learned from my entertainment', I.iv.216–17) she tacitly admits the embarrassment which her own conduct causes her. She also finds herself caught up in a situation in which she acts as servant to a master whom she secretly wishes to marry (an ironic parallel to the social-climbing, and therefore disorderly, behaviour of Malvolio); and that situation further involves her in at least appearing to be disloyal to her master by stealing his mistress from him. Sebastian is also caught up in disorderly behaviour: he acts with naked opportunism in a world that he finds both sane and insane, but which offers him a very advantageous marriage with a beautiful woman who seems 'mad' though able to conduct herself with 'a smooth, discreet, and stable bearing' (IV.iii.19).

Sebastian's breach of decorum, like Viola's, is, of course, the result of temporary circumstances, and as the play moves towards its expected happy ending both brother and sister are restored to the orderly world which the audience knows to be naturally theirs. In outlook and behaviour they are not really comparable with either Sir Toby or Malvolio, but that circumstance can cause them to act, at least for the time being, in an unconventional, even disorderly, fashion is nonetheless significant. Though the consequence is nothing like the radical questioning of accepted order values which takes place in Shakespeare's histories and tragedies, there is a liberating sense of confusion. Conventional distinctions are broken down. Without being made to disapprove of Viola and Sebastian, we see them as characters whose behaviour is at least capable of being thought of as disorderly; and, on the other hand, though continuing to disapprove of Malvolio as one who violates the 'order' code, we see him as in some ways representative of that code. Sir Toby becomes similarly ambivalent – a riotous figure, and yet one who wins our anarchic approval. Most elusive of all, Feste appears as a migrant between the worlds of both order and disorder. The result is a more subtle and malleable apprehension of values than the orthodox standards of 'degree' allow. The comedy is not subversive, but it compels us to adjust to a more flexible and variable reality.

3.5 APPEARANCE AND REALITY

The contrast between appearance and reality is another major preoccupation of this play. Its most obvious manifestation is in the use of disguise. By dressing herself as a boy and taking the name, Cesario, Viola – like several other heroines in Shakespearian comedy – establishes a false appearance which, as suggested above, is both liberating and dangerous. In her role as 'Cesario' she enjoys a freedom of action which is denied her as a woman. (It is also theatrically effective, since in the Elizabethan theatre boys took the part of women, and as a result it is both pleasing to the audience to watch the double-take of a boy playing the part of a girl playing the part of a boy and easier for the boy-actor to perform such a role.) At the same time disguise becomes 'a wickedness' luring Olivia to fall in love with the mere semblance of a man: as Viola remarks, 'she were better love a dream' (II.ii.26–7). Since she cannot make the feminine appeal to Orsino that she would like, Viola herself is also a sufferer; and to add to her distress she must face the ordeal of acting as proxy wooer of another woman. Later, disguise almost involves her in a duel for which her true, feminine nature makes her quite unsuited – though she is saved from that by another freak of false appearance, when at the crucial moment of danger she is mistaken for her brother and rescued by Antonio.

In a more general sense, false appearances also form the basis of the gulling of Malvolio. The letter which is dropped in his path is a forgery, and it is worded so as to encourage him into believing his own fantasies about Olivia. Sir Andrew is likewise gulled by a false image of Olivia's inclinations when Fabian tells him that she showed favour to Viola/Cesario only as a form of provocation: 'You should then have accosted her, and with some excellent jests fire-new from the mint, you should have banged the youth into dumbness. This was looked for at your hand . . . ' (III.ii.21–4). Both deceptions work because both gulls are ripe for gulling: they indulge imaginary notions which are ridiculously wide of reality. Sir Andrew fondly thinks of himself as a witty gallant. Malvolio deceives himself with dreams of power; in II.v, even before he picks up the letter, he has illusions of grandeur: 'Calling my officers about me, in my branched velvet gown, having come from a day-bed, where I have left Olivia sleeping . . . ' (48–50). The letter merely plays upon this existing state of mind; as Sir Toby observes, Maria's device has 'put him in such a dream that when the image of it leaves him he must run mad' (193–4).

The leaving of such images – i.e. the return from deception to truth – is a complementary aspect of the theme of illusion and reality. With Malvolio it is accomplished by carrying illusion itself to excess. The one-man show in which Feste plays both the Fool and the parson, Sir Topas, is a brilliant example of illusion-making, and its final effect is to bring Malvolio back to reality with a bump. To the final riddling question from Feste, 'But tell me true, are you not mad indeed, or do you but counterfeit?' he replies with a simple assertion in the plainest of words: 'Believe me, I am not. I tell thee true' (IV.ii.117–19). And in the final scene, after the deception has been fully exposed, Olivia echoes Malvolio's own phrase when she re- marks to Orsino that 'He hath been most notoriously abused' (V.i.381). In parallel style – though perhaps to be taken less seriously – Sir Andrew's gulling comes to an end with 'a bloody coxcomb' (190) and a final encounter with the blunt, downrightly spoken truth of reality, as Sir Toby abandons all flattery and tells him to his face that he is 'An asshead, and a coxcomb, and a knave – a thin-faced knave, a gull!' (207–8).

Turning to the more romantic areas of the play, we find that the fostering of illusion is, if anything, of even greater significance there. Love, as we have seen, engenders fantastic day-dreams and fantasies, causing Orsino to live in a world of sentimental make-believe and Olivia to play the part – quite unreal for her – of a cloistered nun. Equally, the comic movement away from illusion and towards accommodation to reality is just as evident in their careers. Feste's all-licenced foolery, which makes fun of both characters' self-deceptions, points the way to their eventual recognition of where reality, and true love, lies. Thus in the last Act Orsino claims his 'share in this most happy wrack' (V.i.268), realising perhaps in retrospect that what drew him earlier to 'Cesario' was the feminine reality – that which was 'semblative a woman's part' (I.iv.36) – beneath Viola's disguise; and Sebastian tells Olivia that it was a true instinct which drew her to him, notwithstanding her confusion:

> So comes it, lady, you have been mistook.
> But nature to her bias drew in that –
> You would have been contracted to a maid.
> Nor are you therein, by my life, deceived:
> You are betrothed both to a maid and man. (V.i.261–5)

The rite of passage from illusion to reality is happier for these romantic characters than it is for Malvolio and Sir Andrew – though it is not to be overlooked that some very painful moments are encompassed on the way, and that an almost Othello-like tragedy is threatened by Orsino's 'savage jealousy' before illusion is finally banished (see V.i.117–31). For them illusion is ultimately benevolent. Though her disguise is a 'wickedness', it is also the means by which Viola is able to get past the barrier of Orsino's conventional love-melancholy and form a more vital relationship with him. For Olivia it is a means enabling her to find true love in Sebastian; and for Sebastian himself it becomes a marvellous blessing. His remarkable speech at the beginning of IV.iii is full of a bewilderment which makes him ready to 'distrust' his eyes and think that either he or Olivia is mad, but it also affirms 'This is the air, that is the glorious sun . . . ' and insists on the indisputable evidence of his own senses – 'This pearl she gave me, I do *feel*'t and *see*'t.' In practice he accepts quite cheerfully what opportunity throws his way, even though he knows that some kind of illusion must be responsible for it; and in his final words to Olivia he finds a persuasive rationalisation for illusion – when it is finally revealed to be such – as an agent of reality rather than deception.

Such manifestations of illusion are creative. They enable the prosaic dimension of reality to be transcended. In this respect they are the necessary ally of romance, which also transcends reality through the work of the imagination. But the creativity is validated only if the characters are restored to the real world, where men are men and women are women, and where orderly social relationships obtain. Fortunately, the spirit of comedy ensures that this restoration does take place in *Twelfth Night*. It is, for example, a minor but revealing touch that Orsino reassures Olivia, when she finds that she is actually married, not to 'Cesario' but to Sebastian, that her husband is socially acceptable: 'Be not amazed; right noble is his blood'. Sebastian is a gentleman and therefore the marriage will not be unequal. Had he been an upstart, differing only from Malvolio in being handsome and charming, the wickedness of disguise would have been devastatingly confirmed, for in the real world, particularly the real Elizabethan world, such a misalliance would have been intolerable. As it is, Sebastian's sound social credentials, added to his vigorous masculinity, make him a very suitable husband for Olivia. In meeting and marrying him, albeit while temporarily inhabiting a world of illusion, she has found a solidly real basis for her future life, such as neither her sentimental isolation nor Malvolio's (nor Sir Andrew's) preposterous aspirations could realistically hope to provide.

4 DRAMATIC TECHNIQUES

4.1 SHAKESPEARE'S USE OF HIS SOURCES

Manningham refers to the resemblance between *Twelfth Night* and a comedy 'in Italian called *Inganni*' (see above, p. 4). A play of that name was written by Nicolo Secchi in 1562; but it is *Gl'Ingannati* ('The Deceived'), written by members of the Academy of the Intronati for performance at the Siena Carnival in 1531, which is closer to Shakespeare's plot. *Gl'Ingannati* is a comedy set in Modena, where a brother and sister, Fabrizio and Lelia, are mistaken for each other in similar fashion to Shakespeare's Sebastian and Viola. Lelia has fallen in love with a young man called Flamminio, who has subsequently deserted her for Isabella, the daughter of Gherardo, and to keep near to Flamminio Lelia disguises herself as a page (Fabio) in his service. Flamminio soon places great trust in Fabio and sends 'him' as a messenger to Isabella, who, however, falls in love with the supposed boy. Meanwhile Lelia's father, Virginio, who has lost much of his wealth in the siege of Rome, seeks to marry her to Gherardo, and is puzzled that he cannot find her. He also believes his son, Fabrizio, to have died in Rome, though in fact Fabrizio is still alive and has found his way to Modena. In the course of the action Fabrizio is mistaken for his sister in peculiar circumstances: Gherardo and Virginio, having penetrated Lelia's disguise, decide to seek out 'Fabio' and lock her up in the same room with Isabella; but the person they find and imprison is Fabrizio. Isabella takes Fabrizio for Fabio and allows him to make love to her. Flamminio who has been told by a jealous servant that Fabio has been deceiving him with regard to Isabella, resolves to take revenge on Fabio, but when he realises her true identity and devotion to himself he accepts her as his wife. The confusion of identities is thus cleared up, and the comedy ends with marriages between Flamminio and Lelia and Fabrizio and Isabella. Other characters include Lelia's and Fabrizio's nurse, Clemenzia; a pedant; various servants; and Giglio, a foolish Spaniard, who is duped by Gherardo's maid, Pasquella. The intrigues of these characters form the sub-plot of the play.

Whether Shakespeare had access to a copy of *Gl'Ingannati* and sufficient Italian to construe it, or whether he knew of it by report, is uncertain; all that can be said is that it is a possible source, direct or indirect, for some of the plot features of *Twelfth Night*. In spirit, however, it is very different. In Bullough's words, it is 'an unsentimental, bustling comedy', quite unlike the romantic comedy written by Shakespeare.

Another more probable source, and one more in tune with *Twelfth Night*, is the English story of *Apolonius and Silla* included by Barnaby Riche in his collection, *Riche His Farewell to Militarie Profession* (1581). In this tale Duke Apolonius, of Constantinople, on his way home after fighting against the Turks is driven ashore at Cyprus, where the governor, Duke Pontus, entertains him until his ships are made seaworthy again. During Apolonius's stay Pontus's daughter, Silla, falls in love with him, but is unable to attract his attention. After his departure she resolves to follow him to Constantinople, and for this purpose she enlists the aid of a faithful servant, Pedro. Together they board a ship, but the captain, attracted by her beauty, tries to woo her to be his wife, and when he is rejected threatens to rape her. She is saved, however, by a storm which wrecks the ship and drowns most of the crew, including Pedro. She herself gets to land on one of the captain's sea-chests, and in it she finds some clothing which enables her to dress as a man. In this disguise she reaches Constantinople, where she presents herself to Apolonius, and is taken into his service as a page, using the name of her identical twin, Silvio, who is fighting as a soldier in Africa. Apolonius, who is wooing a noble and wealthy widow, Julina, uses 'Silvio' as his messenger to her. Julina falls in love with the page and will have nothing to do with Apolonius's suit, thus putting Silla in an acutely embarrassing situation. Meanwhile the true Silvio returns to Cyprus, learns of Silla's mysterious disappearance and sets out to search for her. His journeying brings him to Contantinople, where he accidentally encounters Julina, who, taking him for his disguised sister, invites him to supper, persuades him to stay the night and gets herself pregnant by him. Silvio resumes his travels the next day. As a result of servants' gossip Apolonius learns that the false 'Silvio' has become the object of Julina's love and has 'him' thrown into prison. Julina herself, becoming aware of her pregnancy and hearing what has happened to the page, begs Apolonius to release 'him' and to allow their marriage to take place. Silla denies her involvement with Julina, and is only able to convince the latter by revealing that she is a woman disguised as a boy. The outcome is that Apolonius now realises her to be the daughter of Duke Pontus and he is so impressed by her devotion that he falls in love with, and marries, her. Julina is rescued from her plight when news reaches the true Silvio that his sister has been found and he comes back to Constantinople. He admits that it was he who slept with Julina and makes amends by marrying her.

Twelfth Night clearly owes more to *Apolonius and Silla* than to *Gl'Ingannati*, but there are still notable differences. For example, Shakespeare avoids subjecting Olivia (his equivalent for Julina) to the embarrassment of having to admit to premarital sex, and neither of his seamen – the Captain who helps Viola, or Antonio who befriends Sebastian – is made to imitate the lust of the captain who tries to rape Silla. Riche's characters utter rhetorical speeches of elaborate sentiment, but it is Shakespeare who gives them the psychology and enchanting language of romance. On the other hand, there is an element of bawdiness and grossness in Shakespeare, primarily associated with the low-life episodes in *Twelfth Night*, which is absent from Riche, who writes for a readership of middle-class women; and for these scenes *Gl'Ingannati* is a more plausible influence than *Apolonius and Silla*. However, there is very little precise connection between the action of the sub-plot of *Gl'Ingannati* and that of *Twelfth Night*. Sir Toby, Sir Andrew, Maria, Fabian and Feste are all Shakespeare's own invention, and apart from the topical elements suggested by Hotson (see above, p. 3), there are no models for the character of Malvolio and the plot against him. The adroit way in which the low-life business is made to interact with the Orsino–Viola–Olivia–Sebastian story is likewise Shakespeare's own invention – though not something without precedent in his own work in that such relationship between main plot and sub-plot is characteristic of almost all his foregoing comedies.

Disguise, especially in the form of a young woman adopting the role of a boy, is also typical of earlier comedies such as *The Two Gentleman of Verona*, *The Merchant of Venice* and *As You Like It*, and mistaken identity is as much, if not more, the basis of the comedy in *The Comedy of Errors* as it is in *Twelfth Night*. In these respects one of the principal sources for *Twelfth Night* is Shakespeare's own previous work. He does not merely repeat himself, but he certainly plays variations on themes which he has used before; and for readers and audiences familiar with his earlier work there is an added pleasure in recognising this.

4.2 PLOT AND STRUCTURE

The balancing of a high-life by a low-life plot is a common feature of Shakespearian comedy. In *A Midsummer Night's Dream*, for example, the confusions of the lovers, Hermia, Lysander, Helena and Demetrius, are offset by the farcical story of the attempt by Bottom and his fellow-Athenian workmen to present the tragedy of 'Pyramus and Thisby'. This structure is used again in *Twelfth Night*, but in this play there is a doubling up of both high- and low-life elements. Orsino's wooing of Olivia, with Viola/Cesario as his proxy, and Sebastian's involvement with Olivia as a result of being mistaken for 'Cesario' become the two strands constituting the high-life plot; and the gullings of Malvolio and Sir Andrew Aguecheek respectively provide the twin elements of the low-life plot. As is also customary in Shakespearian comedy, these double strands are not kept separate, but are interwoven. Thus Olivia figures as the desired lady in both the Orsino and Sebastian plots, and Viola is likewise an essential element in both. In the gulling of Malvolio Sir Toby is one of the prime movers (though Maria is the actual inventor of the letter-trick) while Sir Andrew tags along as a rather naively stupid assistant; and it is also Sir Toby who urges Sir Andrew to keep on with his hopeless suit to Olivia and who plays the major part in arranging the preposterous duel between Sir Andrew and 'Cesario'. In addition, there is inter-action between the high-life and low-life plots in that Olivia is the subject of the attentions of all four wooers – Orsino, Sebastian, Malvolio and Sir Andrew; and, helping to weave the various strands more closely together, Viola plays at least some part in all four plots, as well as herself becoming a reluctant fifth contender for Olivia's hand. (Without Viola, indeed, Sebastian could not be reckoned one of the number, since it is his resemblance to his boyishly-clad sister which leads to his involvement.) The other character who appears in all four plots is Feste. He darts in and out of the various scenes, joining in the boon companionship of the low-life characters such as Sir Toby, Maria and Fabian, performing his professional fooling and singing at the behest of his social superiors, Orsino and Olivia, having encounters with Viola and Sebastian and mocking Malvolio (though not playing a part in the letter business). Compared with Viola he is a less involved character – he is often, indeed, rather coolly detached in his relations with others. But his ubiquity helps to maintain the impression of the play as an interconnected, if not closely integrated, whole.

Besides these four interwoven plots there is also the story of the shipwreck of Viola and Sebastian, their separation and their final reunion. In the service of this plot two other, quite different, characters, Antonio and the Captain, make brief appearances. With them a whiff of the sea, and a sense of the potentially tragic uncertainty attending seafaring life, penetrate an otherwise seemingly courtly, landlocked setting. Their impact is chiefly near the beginning and the end of the play – Antonio, it is true, appears in II.i, III.iii, III.iv (entering at line 321) and V.i, but it is as the rescuer of Sebastian from the shipwreck which opens the play and as intended rescuer for a second time at the height of the duel episode that he makes his chief contributions. The Captain appears near the beginning only (I.ii), again in the immediate aftermath of the shipwreck, and is mentioned in V.i.276–80 as having been imprisoned 'at Malvolio's suit'. Through them Viola and Sebastian are brought to Illyria – transferred from one kind of uncertainty (the sea) to another (the confusions and illusions of Illyria); they then recede into the background for most of the central section of the play; and they are recalled towards to the end. In musical terms their effect is like that of a prelude and a coda; and they also hint at a wider world of suffering and hardship outside the enclosed Illyrian world.

Nonetheless, if the little life of *Twelfth Night* is rounded with the sea (to adapt words from *The Tempest*, which also uses shipwreck and a similar opening and closing device), it is a sufficiently complex and rapidly shifting life to hold the audience's fascinated attention. The interacting elements of the plot work together to produce parallels and contrasts, changes of atmosphere and a dazzling succession of dramatic images which give an impression of great fluency and variety. The controlling of the pace of the action is especially important in creating this impression. The opening scene is leisurely, almost languid, as a richly plangent music is played and Orsino broods on his love-melancholy. The second is less atmospheric, but for that reason an effective contrast, and tells us about serious matters of shipwreck rather than self-indulgent fantasies. In it we also see an afflicted character (Viola) being active – as far as her situation will allow – rather than passive. I.iii is a still more downright contrast, opening with Sir Toby's dismissive bluntness and going on to the boozy baiting of Sir Andrew which is as remote as may be from the plaintiveness of Orsino. By I.iv the action has already begun to develop – Viola/Cesario is well in favour with the Duke; and in I.v not only is her role as messenger to Olivia seen in action (with its startling effect on Olivia), but the different moods and tones associated with Feste and Malvolio are blended into the mixture. The gathering momentum is interrupted briefly at the opening of Act II to allow Sebastian's situation to be communicated to the audience; but II.ii develops the absorbing relationship between Olivia and Viola, and in II.iii the hatching of a scheme for deceiving Malvolio stirs up the audience's expectations of something to laugh at in later scenes. Time is again given to romantic sentiment in II.iv (with suitably atmospheric music), but thereafter the action is scarcely allowed to slacken. The brilliantly farcical letter-scene (II.v) is followed by III.i, in which Olivia throws caution to the winds and declares her love for Cesario. This in turn is followed by the initiation of the duel episode as Sir Andrew's artificially stimulated riposte to the favour now being accorded Cesario. Although the Sebastian/Antonio exchange at III.iii appears to be a slight diversion from the various lines of development which have been set going at this point, these are fully exploited in II.iv with Malvolio's cross-gartered encounter with Olivia and the delivery of Sir Andrew's challenge; and before this scene is concluded II.iii proves to have been the source of a still more exciting complication of the duel business as Antonio mistakes Viola/Cesario for Sebastian. The pace rapidly accelerates in Act IV, with a complementary mistaking of Sebastian for Cesario which costs Andrew a drubbing and Toby disgrace in the eyes of Olivia for attacking Sebastian/Cesario; a second phase to the Malvolio gulling in the form of the Sir Topas episode; and the lightning love-match between Sebastian and Olivia. A little fooling between Feste and Orsino serves as a momentary breathing-space at the beginning of Act V, but then the action races to its climax: Antonio's danger is pushed to one side by the audience's much greater concern for the danger of Viola caught in an impossible situation between Orsino and Olivia; Andrew and Toby display their bloody coxcombs; and at last the presence of Sebastian and Viola on the stage together resolves the central difficulty, releases the tension and makes the comedy's happy ending possible. Finally, however, the acerbity of Malvolio's exit and Feste's song round the play off on a slightly disconcerting, though not too sharply discordant, note.

4.3 CHARACTERISATION

As in consideration of the structure, the *dramatis personae* (dramatic personages) of *Twelfth Night* may be divided into high-life and low-life characters. To the first group belong Orsino, Olivia, Viola and Sebastian; to the second Sir Toby Belch, Sir Andrew Aguecheek, Maria, Fabian, Malvolio and Feste – though in the tradition of the 'licensed' fool Feste is allowed to mingle with the high-life characters as well (hence, in part, Malvolio's resentment of him). Antonio, however, cannot easily be placed in either category. The other minor characters, such as Valentine, Curio, the First and Second Officers, etc., are what in modern film parlance would be called 'extras' – i.e. functionaries whose social status is defined by the other figures among whom they appear, and whose characterisation is relatively unimportant.

Orsino, Duke of Illyria, is at the apex of this society. He enjoys supreme political power, and we see something of his political role when, for example, Antonio is brought before him accused of capturing certain Illyrian vessels and causing a sea-fight in which 'your [Orsino's] young nephew Titus lost his leg' (V.i.62) – a point which might be expected particularly to tell against Antonio in the judgement to be passed upon him. But for most of the play this aspect of Orsino is in abeyance. To the audience he is primarily the lovesick Petrarchan lover in the conventional posture of beseeching adoration of Olivia. A somewhat literary idea of love seems to dominate him, and he is fond of the appropriate accoutrements of sentimental music and extravagantly 'poetic' language. To this extent he is an undeveloped character. However, he is more than just a handsome poseur (which is, presumably, why Viola falls in love with him). When not wrapped in his own egotism he can be perceptive and sympathetic, as when he recognises the essential femininity of 'Cesario' (I.iv.31–8), and he is sensible in the advice he gives on the need for a man to marry a woman younger than himself (II.iv.29–5). (Modern feminists may not approve of this, but it would certainly have received approval in Elizabethan times. And in any case Orsino must be given credit for going against merely received opinion when he asserts that it is men who are 'giddy and unfirm' rather than women.) These are hints of a capacity for better understanding and wisdom which his contact with Cesario seems to draw out. As Ruth Nevo suggests, his response to Cesario 'brings out in Orsino a new, mature and manly good sense' (*Comic Transformations in Shakespeare*, p. 208). Even his outburst of jealousy in V.i is evidence of improvement, for it is provoked by more passionate feeling than that which goes with his previously artificial sentiment; and his shrewd acknowledgement that Viola has already tacitly declared her love for him – 'Boy, thou hast said to me a thousand times/Thou never shouldst love woman like to me' (V.i.269–70) sets a quiet seal to their relationship which is more eloquent than his earlier rhetoric.

Olivia may be regarded as the female counterpart of Orsino in that she, too, is drawn out of affectation (disproportionate grief over her brother's death) into a turbulent, but more healthy, passion of love. 'Passion' is not perhaps the right word, as her falling in love with Cesario is more in the nature of infatuation than a profound love experience. It does, however, release dangerously pent-up emotions, and by responding as she does to the pert boldness and ready tongue of the seeming boy Olivia is at least showing her appreciation of spirited individuality. She is a lady who values propriety – hence her (qualified) approval of Malvolio, and, as Sebastian recognises, she is one who conducts her affairs in an orderly and responsible manner (IV.iii.16–20); but, as the terms of her rejection of Orsino show (I.v.260–6), she needs more than formal accomplishments and social status in the man who is to rouse her deepest feelings. The vitality she senses in Viola is something which she instinctively recognises as necessary to her fulfilment; and Viola/Cesario becomes the catalyst enabling Olivia to find this essential quality in Sebastian. Although romance favours 'love at first sight', and to that extent there is no need to justify her sudden acceptance of Sebastian, Olivia's response to Cesario not only provides an excuse based on mistaken identity, but also prepares the way psychologically for the later relationship. For in general Olivia does not seem a flighty, headstrong woman. Nor is she lacking in warm feeling and understanding. Her sympathetic tolerance of Feste shows her to be a sensible woman who knows the value of witty but perceptive criticism. She herself is a wise critic of Malvolio; she knows both his good and his bad qualities; and when she understands the tricks that have been played upon him she shows reasonable, though not sentimentally excessive, compassion. By the end of the play she is ready for marriage in the best comic manner, but her 'happy ending' is no more than a confirmation of her innate vitality and good sense.

Viola is the romantic heroine, but thanks to her disguise she is able to enjoy a far more active role than might otherwise be the case. As with the heroines of *The Merchant of Venice* (Portia) and *As You Like It* (Rosalind), her persona as a boy releases the pert, witty, assertive side of her character. It is this attractive boyishness which captivates Olivia. Her ready answers show a kind of charming swagger which spreads to her whole being, as Olivia recognises when she broods on Cesario's words:

> 'What is your parentage?'
> 'Above my fortunes, yet my state is well.
> I am a gentleman.' I'll be sworn thou art!
> Thy tongue, thy face, thy limbs, actions, and spirit
> Do give thee fivefold blazon. (I.v.292–6)

Yet Viola retains her femininity as well. This is apparent to Orsino, even when he takes her for a boy:

> For they shall yet belie thy happy years
> That say thou art a man. Diana's lip

Is not more smooth and rubious. Thy small pipe
Is as the maiden's organ, shrill and sound,
And all is semblative a woman's part. (I.iv.32–6)

And, of course, she shows feminine timidity when it comes to the
prospect of fighting a duel. Although she shows both a capacity for
quick intuitive action – for example, in seizing the opportunity to
serve the Duke 'as an eunuch' (I.ii.43–4) and in perceiving the effect
of her Cesario persona on Olivia – she is also well aware of the
limitations still imposed on her freedom of action by her sex. At the
same time she possesses a vibrancy and depth of emotion which
perhaps belong to her essential womanliness, but which her masculine role enables her to express with unusual frankness. This gives
rise to some of the most resonant speeches in the play – for example,
'Make me a willow cabin at your gate' (I.v.271–9), in which she
adopts the conventional posture of the Petrarchan lover with his
'loyal cantons of contemned love', but through the force of her
sympathetic imagination turns it into something movingly real; and
'She sat like Patience on a monument' (II.iv.110–18), in which she
creates an allegory revealing the depth of frustration and suffering
resulting from what is in effect her own situation. The contrast
between her appearance of bright, spritely male youthfulness and this
almost tragic femininity is symptomatic of her double nature, which
consists of both practical energy and deep feeling. In this sense she is
simultaneously masculine and feminine; and her disguise is not only
an effective plot device, but also a means of displaying the full range
of her virtually androgynous character.

Viola's brother, *Sebastian*, is her identical twin and, as such, may
be regarded as another manifestation of her masculine persona.
Certainly, that is how Olivia – albeit unwittingly – responds to him;
and perhaps the correspondingly feminine aspect of his personality
(that which corresponds to the 'Viola' in him, as he corresponds to
the 'Cesario' in Viola) has something to do with the strong affection
which Antonio feels for him. However, he is predominantly the
traditionally romantic hero, handsome, generous, noble and brave –
though also, it must be said, something of an opportunist in his
readiness to accept Olivia's unexpected advances. Nonetheless, he is
not unscrupulous; his response to Olivia is one of instant commitment
and loyalty, and in his relationship with Antonio he displays a
warmth and spontaneity which makes the latter's sense of betrayal all
the greater when he confuses brother and sister in III.iv. But
Sebastian's character does not involve the rich complexity of Viola.

In the main he is simply the young male 'lead' without whom a romantic comedy would be incomplete.

Sir Andrew Aguecheek and Sir Toby Belch are 'low-life' characters despite their titles. *Sir Andrew* has social pretensions, and Sir Toby constantly flatters him by addressing him as 'knight', but his notion of cutting a figure in society is to attend 'masques and revels', indulge in clever banter with women and drink till the early hours of the morning – in short, to gain a reputation as 'a gallant'. Even in these dubious pursuits, however, he is a hopeless dunce, and he has no idea how far he falls short of competence – let alone excellence. Sir Toby can pretend to praise him, while satirising him mercilessly (see, for example, Sir Toby's speech, 'Wherefore are these things hid? . . . ', I.iii.125–33), secure in the knowledge that Sir Andrew lacks the wit to appreciate what a fool he is being made to appear. Indeed, anyone can score off Sir Andrew; and to complete his total inadequacy as a 'knight' he is a thorough coward. As Maria says, 'besides that he's a fool, he's a great quarreller; and but that he hath the gift of a coward to allay the gust he hath in quarrelling, 'tis thought among the prudent he would quickly have the gift of a grave' (I.iii.29–33). Yet the very naiveté of Sir Andrew (plus the fact that the only one to suffer from his folly is himself) saves him from being merely contemptible, and makes him to some degree likeable. His vanity is silly, rather than vicious; and his almost complete lack of self-criticism lends him a kind of disarming innocence. He is invariably a great success on the stage – an object of derision, but also amusingly pathetic in his hopeless longing for approval.

Sir Toby is altogether tougher, wittier and braver than Sir Andrew, but he also demeans his knighthood by his disorderly behaviour and the ruthlessness of his exploitation of Sir Andrew. The contrast between his pretended friendship with Sir Andrew and Antonio's true devotion to Sebastian – Sir Toby squeezing all the money he can out of his dupe, while Antonio generously gives his purse to Sebastian – makes its own unspoken comment. Yet there is no doubt that Sir Toby also wins an indulgent reception from the audience. His laid-back camaraderie, and particularly his resentment of the straight-laced hypocrisy of Malvolio, strike a response from the anti-authoritarian instinct which is present in all of us. He is the principal representative of that 'Twelfth Night' rejection of discipline and restraint which is especially felt in the low-life scenes of carousing and gulling. Like Falstaff (in the *Henry IV* plays) he acts as a safety-valve for the repressed rebelliousness which seethes beneath the decorous surface of an order-conscious society. Consequently, he gets away with what would otherwise have to be condemned as boorish and selfish behaviour (though not entirely, since at the end of the play he, as well as Sir Andrew, receives a 'bloody coxcomb'). In satirical comedy sharp-witted, jovial characters like Sir Toby enjoy a natural advantage, since they are in tune with that common-sense antipathy to pretentiousness which the majority of the audience feels. *Twelfth Night*, however, is a comedy which is more than satirical. It is mixed with romance as well, and in this richer context Sir Toby looks a little coarse and vulgar. He belongs with the 'tosspots' of Feste's closing song, and though he remains deservedly popular with the audience, he is also seen to have his limitations as both a knight and a friend.

Malvolio, like Sir Andrew, is the butt of comedy. He is an almost Jonsonian figure in this otherwise very Shakespearian play. His very name, with its suggestion of 'ill will', echoes the morally labelling names that Jonson gives his characters (e.g. 'Volpone' = the cunning 'fox'; 'Voltore' = the greedy 'vulture', etc.). He is an overweening egotist, a social climber, a hypocrite and an offensive rebuker of others for their slack behaviour. He sounds like one of the Puritans who in Elizabethan times were beginning to make their extremist views heard and were unpopular because of their disapproval of all kinds of merry-making (including attendance at theatres). Maria, however, refuses to dignify him with the theological and moral consistency of a real Puritan: to her:

> The devil a Puritan that he is, or anything, constantly, but a time-pleaser, an affectioned ass that cons state without book and utters it by great swarths; the best persuaded of himself, so crammed, as he thinks, with excellencies, that it is his grounds of faith that all that look on him love him (II.iii.151–6).

These words provide a ready-made thumb-nail sketch of Malvolio's character, and are designed, no doubt, to influence the audience's attitude towards him as a prelude to the letter-trick (the words quoted, emphasising his extravagant conceit, are rounded off with the comment: 'and on that vice in him will my revenge find notable cause to work'). By his actual behaviour he shows that much of what Maria says is justified; but this is not the whole story. If Olivia likewise criticizes him – and to his face ('O, you are sick of self-love', I.v.92), she also speaks of him as being 'sad and civil' (i.e. serious and sedate) and accordingly an appropriate servant for her (III.iv.4–5), and at the end of the play she tacitly recognises that he has been done wrong (V.i.354–7). Much depends on the way an actor chooses to play this role; there have been many different interpretations in the theatre, ranging from vainglorious folly to almost manic self-righteousness. Malvolio's utter conviction that the way he construes the letter is the right one ('Daylight and champain [open country] discovers not more! . . . I do not now fool myself, to let imagination jade me . . . ', II.v.161–5) exposes him to complete ridicule, but the tenor of his replies to 'Sir Topas' – for example, his rejection of the Pythagorean doctrine of the transmigration of souls ('I think nobly of the soul, and no way approve his opinion;, IV.ii.55–6) – reinstates him as a sensible, clear-minded man. The bitterness of his last exit line hints at another dimension as well – that of the persecuted member of a minority sect, which is capable of arousing a certain degree of sympathy. Malvolio is thus a complex character, rather than the one-dimensional figure of Jonsonian satire, and as with all such characters, there is a touch of mystery about him. We see the absurd surface, but we are given hints of a possibly more frustrated, tormented personality lurking beneath.

The minor characters, *Maria* and *Fabian*, represent down-to-earth wit and sanity in a world that can be romantically bewildering and confusing, or preposterously farcical. Sir Toby loves Maria for these qualities (insofar as he can be regarded as capable of love) and is prepared to marry her. Just how much she is to be trusted, however, is doubtful. Her execution of the letter-trick involves her in forging her mistress's handwriting, and if she is willing to practise this much deception to please Sir Toby, her loyalty is uncertain. On the other hand, her deception is perhaps simply a part of her innate liveliness. In any case, we do not really question her motives. It is enough that she and Fabian carry out their part of the plot as agreeable extroverts. What they do matters more than what they are.

Last, but certainly not least, *Feste* is at once the most complex and the most opportunist character of them all. He is the professional Fool, which means that he earns his living by making others laugh. This he does primarily by his wit, especially his play on words, and his agility in argument and repartee. There are two classes of funny men in Shakespearian comedy: the 'clown' who provokes laughter by his ignorance or stupidity (like the 'rude mechanicals' in *A Midsummer Night's Dream* or Dogberry and Verges in *Much Ado About Nothing*), and the Fool, or jester, whose nimble intelligence enables him to be a penetrating analyst of the folly of those around him (like Touchstone in *As You Like It* or the Fool in *King Lear*). Feste belongs emphatically to the second class. He is an employee, dependent on his employer's (in this case, Olivia's) favour, but free, within limits, to take material for his fooling from anyone he sees, including his social superiors. Malvolio considers him merely 'a barren rascal' who has to be humoured: 'unless you laugh and minister occasion to him, he is gagged' (I.v.85–9). Olivia, however, detects that Malvolio's censure is provoked by the discomfort he feels – presumably from some of the sharp things that Feste has said about him. In her opinion 'There is no slander in an allowed fool, though he do nothing but rail; nor no railing in a known discreet man, though he do nothing but reprove' (95–8). In other words, the laughter provoked will only sting if the criticism has hit a target. This defines Feste's role admirably, as Feste himself acknowledges ('Now Mercury endue thee with leasing, for thou speak'st well of fools', 99–100). To perform this function, however, requires exceptional adroitness, as Viola – an equally eloquent defender of Fools – testifies at III.i.61–70, and as Feste demonstrates by daring to expose the folly of Orsino, and even that of his own mistress, but in such a way as to win their applause rather than provoke their annoyance. That he does not succeed with Malvolio perhaps shows the limits of his tact, or, more plausibly, reveals Malvolio's inability to understand such a rare combination of subservience and insubordination. (The fact that Feste refuses to regard him as a social superior very probably has something to do with it as well.)

Besides this, Feste is also a singer, able to produce from his professional repertoire just the kind of musical love-melancholy, with appropriate words ('Come away, come away, death'), that will suit Orsino's mood, or a song of 'good life' for Sir Toby and Sir Andrew (in II.iii) which suits their total immersion in the pleasure of the moment. Neither of these can be relied on as an index to Feste's own feelings; but 'When that I was and a little tiny boy', the song which he sings alone on the stage, and as epilogue to the whole play, possibly does reveal more of himself. It adds a wary note of disenchantment to the perpetual role-playing that the Fool's vocation involves, suggesting that folly and knavery belong to each time of life, but that rain and storm are the most recurrent features. Yet the player must continue playing, and strive to please his audience every day. Private anxieties – which in Feste's case may include the fear of losing his job and the humiliation of defeat in professional competition (see I.v.16–17 and 85–7) – have to be put aside: 'the show must go on'. If there is a touch of mystery in Malvolio's character, this is even more marked in Feste's. We know very little of the real person behind the entertainer and multifarious role-player. At the most there are hints of insecurity gnawing at an otherwise confidently sophisticated professional persona; but these are enough to give an impression of greater psychological depth. When he says to Olivia, 'Thou hast spoke for us, madonna, as if thy eldest son should be a fool . . .'

(I.v.114–15), he expresses his gratitude in a phrase that has curiously religious overtones. For the most part this Fool is anything but a pious one, and here, no doubt, he hides behind the mocking manner of expression allowed by his vocation. The suggestion, however, of an analogy between Olivia and himself and the Madonna and Child may reveal a truth, as jests can, about Feste's need for protection and comfort in a harsh world. Though he is the most detached professional in the play there is still within him an element of the 'little tiny boy' who must strive to please his audience every day.

4.4 LANGUAGE

Word-play, or punning, is endemic in Elizabethan literature, and Shakespeare is entirely a man of his age in making extensive use of it, especially in his comedies. As Feste exclaims, after an elaborate exchange with Viola/Cesario in which the phrase 'live by' is teased into three different meanings, 'To see this age! A sentence is but a cheveril glove to a good wit; how quickly the wrong side may be turned outward!' (II.i.11–13). Such verbal quibbling is frequently no more than a deliberate exercise in linguistic self-consciousness, which no one is expected to take seriously; but it may also be part of intensely emotional speech, as in the absurd, yet, as far as Orsino is concerned, passionately intended pun on hart/heart in I.i. Whichever category a particular example may belong to is less important than the overall effect of the slippery and unpredictable nature of language, coupled with the sense that one needs to be very agile mentally to survive without loss of face in the company of such expert manipulators of words. In this respect the prevalence of puns is a verbal counterpart to the theme of illusion and reality. It is necessary to keep one's wits about one in a world composed of such ambiguity both of appearances and meanings.

From another point of view, however, word-play reflects the flexibility and variety implicit in romantic comedy, which is similarly expressed in the highly metaphorical nature of Shakespeare's language. This device, by which one thing is expressed in terms of another, demands considerable mental agility and the imagination to perceive resemblances, or connections, in seemingly disparate material. *Twelfth Night* opens with a speech of this kind. In Orsino's brooding comment on the music which is being played the abstraction, 'love', is treated as if it were a living creature requiring food for its existence, and, still more strangely, that food is said to be 'music' (fed, perhaps, through the ear!). The metaphor is then continued through the next two lines, as its possibilities are extended to include a wilful excess leading to 'surfeiting' and so to loss of appetite. In the process the notion of sickness is also introduced, and through this imaginative exploration listening to music becomes an analogy for the extravagance inherent in a self-indulgent attitude to love.

Elsewhere the verbal connections are expressed in the form of simile (where the comparison is made explicit) – as, for example, in Viola's statement that her 'sister' never told her love, but let it secretly undermine her life 'like a worm'i'th'bud'; or in the form of personification (but including simile as well) as in the further comment that: 'She sat like Patience on a monument/Smiling at grief' (II.iv.110–15). This distinction, however, is not an important one. The metaphorical mode of expression is so pervasive in Shakespeare that literal and extended meanings constantly merge into each other. For example, when Orsino comments that Cesario's voice is like a woman's, he says: 'Thy small pipe/Is as the maiden's organ, shrill and sound' (I.iv.34–5). The 'as' in these words indicates a comparison, and the simplest paraphrase would be: 'Thy small windpipe produces a high-pitched sound like that produced by a maiden's voice.' But 'pipe' and 'organ' both have musical overtones (assisted by the recurrent references to music which are also a notable feature of the language of this play), so that there are metaphorical implications as well, suggesting that Cesario's voice is connected by Orsino with the sound of a woodwind instrument, which is further associated with the treble sound of a maiden's voice.

Another example, again with a musical implication, occurs when Viola declares her intention to present herself as an eunuch to Orsino ('for I can sing/And speak to him in many sorts of music') and the Captain says, in a slightly fanciful way, that he will keep her secret:

Be you his eunuch, and your mute I'll be.
When my tongue blabs, then let mine eyes not see. (I.ii.60–1)

Viola means that she will present herself at the Duke's court as a castrato singer, presumably because this will help to account for her high voice despite her male appearance. But in using the word 'mute' the Captain does not mean that he will pretend to be one of those dumb servants that oriental potentates chose to have around them (they could hear, but not give away their master's secrets); he is simply taking up Viola's 'eunuch' reference and extending it by a witty metaphor to include himself as a confidant in whom she can have complete trust. Such language, like punning, is particularly apt for a play full of disguises, illusions and transmutations. It is the language of Illyria – a place name which evokes a typical play on words from Viola when she first hears it used: 'And what should I do in Illyria?/My brother, he is in Elysium' (I.ii.3–4). The phonic similarity of 'Illyria' and 'Elysium' points a contrast between the scene of the present action and the heaven where Viola thinks her drowned brother has gone; but it also associates the two, so that a kind of subdued metaphor connects the real and the mythical place. This metaphorical connection is, in a curious way, further substantiated by the fact that Sebastian is not dead, but as much in Illyria as Viola. Hence 'He is in Elysium' effects what is at least a verbal equation between Illyria and Elysium, reinforcing their imaginative interchangeability. And to cap the ingenious confusion, the audience is, of course, aware that Viola is not standing on the shore of the Mediterranean Illyria, but on the platform of the Globe theatre temporarily metamorphosed by the imagination into that romantically distant maritime country, the 'Illyria' of *Twelfth Night*.

Further contributions to this sense of confusion between the real and the imaginary come from the play's references to dreams and madness. At the conclusion of the letter-scene, in which Malvolio has been persuaded – and has done even more to persuade himself – that he is the beloved of Olivia, Sir Toby compliments Maria by telling her that she has put Malvolio 'in such a dream that when the image of it leaves him he must run mad' (II.v.193–4). Again in IV.i, Sebastian, having just been attacked by Sir Andrew and Sir Toby and then treated astonishingly kindly by Olivia, expresses his bewilderment with the words:

> Or I am mad, or else this is a dream.
> Let fancy still my sense in Lethe steep;
> If it be thus to dream, still let me sleep! (IV.i.61–3)

In the first of these two quotations the primary meaning of 'run mad' is that in waking from dream to reality Malvolio will be wild with anger, but the sense of insanity is also present, suggesting that the transition will actually be from one form of delusion to another. In the second, although Sebastian thinks he must be either insane or dreaming, he prefers this state – which includes the devotion of such an eligible lady – to what ordinary, waking reality has to offer. Other allusions to madness include IV.iii.10–16, which again expresses Sebastian's bewilderment; V.i.67 and 98, referring to Antonio's strange behaviour; and V.i.283, which couples Malvolio's seeming madness with the 'extracting [= distracting] frenzy' which caused it to be banished from Olivia's mind. And in addition to these Feste's 'Sir Topas' trick completes the virtual breakdown of ordinary distinctions between sanity and insanity by enacting a play-within-the play of madness. It is not surprising, therefore, that Sebastian exclaims, 'Are all the people mad?' (IV.i.27). In such a world of mistaken identities, romantic extravagances, deceptions and inversions of normality, extending into the word-play and metaphorical expressions which its inhabitants habitually employ, the logic of the dreamer/madman seems almost as prevalent as it is in *Alice in Wonderland*.

The setting of this world of dream and madness is on land – though the capital city which appears to be the location of the action is probably a seaport. Most of the scenes are indoors, or in a garden, or in a street. But a connection with the sea is recurrently suggested; and, again, primarily through the play's language. The plot depends on a shipwreck which has divided sister from brother so that neither knows of the other's survival, and therefore in I.ii and II.i, where information regarding this shipwreck is communicated to the audience, references to the sea are inevitable. Through images and allusions, however, the sense of sea and shipwreck permeates the rest of the play as well. For example, the sea forms part of Orsino's metaphorical language at I.i.10–11 and II.iv.100, and it enters, again metaphorically, into the comically swashbuckling exchange between Maria and Viola/Cesario at I.v.204–6 ('Will you hoist sail, sir? . . . No, good swabber, I am to hull here a little longer') and the similarly mocking metaphor used by Fabian to Sir Andrew at III.i.26–7 ('you are now sailed into the north of my lady's opinion'). Moreover, the drowning which Viola and Sebastian each fear to have been the fate of the other is not only echoed in serious contexts – by Viola at III.iv.397–8, Antonio at V.i.77–9 and Sebastian at V.i.230–1, but also receives more trivially comic treatment from Feste at I.v.133–5. Finally, the play's happy ending, tragi-comically plucked out of the emotional storms which gather during the central action, is again expressed in appropriately paradoxical sea language, as Orsino claims his long-suffering bride: 'I shall have share in this most happy wrack' (V.i.268).

The effect of these verbal details is perhaps little more than subliminal, but they help to create something of that atmosphere of uncertainty and mystery which naturally belongs to the sea and bring it into the more prosaic world of the land. Like the recurrent references to dream and madness they tend to subvert common-sense assumptions on which ordinary comedy is based and give *Twelfth Night* another, richer dimension.

62

4.5 MUSIC AND SONG

Music is the first sound to reach the audience when a performance of
Twelfth Night begins. It precedes the words; and when words are
spoken they immediately refer to the music. The play likewise ends
with music, in the form of a song from Feste. In between, music is
frequently performed or mentioned: Viola says that she will present
herself to Orsino as a eunuch, 'for I can sing/And speak to him in
many sorts of music' (I.ii.55–6); and when in her role as proxy wooer
she speaks of making 'a willow cabin' at Olivia's gate, she adds that she
would 'Write loyal cantons of contemned love/And sing them loud
even in the dead of night' (I.v.271–4). At Sir Toby's and Sir Andrew's
request Feste sings the 'love song' which begins, 'O mistress mine!
Where are you roaming?' (II.iii.39–52), and this is followed by the
'catch' (or round) which earns the noisy revellers a stern rebuke from
Malvolio; at the beginning of II.iv Orsino again calls for music, which
is a prelude to another song from Feste, 'Come away, come away,
death'; the dialogue between Viola/Cesario and Feste in III.i opens
with the greeting, 'Save thee, friend, and thy music. Does thou live
by thy tabor?'; and in the scene where Malvolio is treated as a
madman Feste sings snatches of songs which help to distinguish his
Fool's role from his role as Sir Topas (IV.ii.73–80, 124–31).

This recurrent use of music may well have been due to the presence
of Robert Armin in the company of actors to which Shakespeare
belonged. Armin was an excellent musician, and Shakespeare may
have deliberately maximised the element of song to give him ample
opportunity to show his paces. Moreover, the audience liked and
expected such entertainment; it helped to make the production a
box-office success. But music is more than a gratuitous addition to
the text of the play. It is an integral part of action and atmosphere.
The ultra-romantic scenes, especially those involving Orsino, would
not be as luxurious and languid as they are without the help of music
and song; and music also contributes something to that enrichment of
atmosphere which, as we have seen, is created by references to
dreams, madness and the sea.

However, the music can be boisterous as well as mellifluous. It is
the accompaniment to eating, drinking and raucous merrymaking,
and as such it represents the pervasive theme of festivity – that
'Twelfth Night' spirit of licence, liberty and letting-your-hair-down
which is anathema to Malvolio. Sir Toby's reply to the steward's
haughty manner of conveying Olivia's displeasure is to take the word
'farewell' ('she is very willing to bid you farewell', III.ii.103–4) as a
cue for an entirely disrespectful song: 'Farewell, dear heart, since I

must needs be gone'; and Feste's song in IV.ii – 'Hey Robin, jolly Robin!/Tell me how thy lady does' – is clearly intended to taunt Malvolio for his pretensions towards Olivia. It is significant that Malvolio himself neither sings nor shows any liking for music. The whole realm of sensibility to which music appeals is alien to him, whether it be romantic or hedonistic. His tense egotism cannot respond to the warm expansiveness of music; but this warm expansiveness is the very element in which *Twelfth Night* thrives. It is a play both penetrated and surrounded with music, which helps to give it its distinctively generous feeling.

5 SPECIMEN PASSAGE

AND

COMMENTARY

Specimen passage

Music plays

ORSINO   Come hither, boy. If ever thou shalt love,
In the sweet pangs of it remember me.
For such as I am, all true lovers are:
Unstaid and skittish in all motions else
Save in the constant image of the creature
That is beloved. How dost thou like this tune?   20

VIOLA   It gives a very echo to the seat
Where love is throned.

ORSINO   Thou dost speak masterly.
My life upon't, young though thou art, thine eye
Hath stayed upon some favour that it loves.
Hath it not, boy?

VIOLA   A little, by your favour.

ORSINO   What kind of woman is't?

VIOLA   Of your complexion.

ORSINO   She is not worth thee, then. What years, i'faith?

VIOLA   About your years, my lord.

ORSINO   Too old, by heaven. Let still the woman take
An elder than herself; so wears she to him;   30
So sways she level in her husband's heart.
For, boy, however we do praise ourselves,
Our fancies are more giddy and unfirm,
More longing, wavering, sooner lost and worn,
Than women's are.

VIOLA   I think it well, my lord.

ORSINO   Then let thy love be younger than thyself,
Or thy affection cannot hold the bent.

> For women are as roses whose fair flower,
> Being once displayed, doth fall that very hour.

VIOLA   And so they are. Alas, that they are so,   40
> To die, even when they to perfection grow.

(II.iv.15–41)

Commentary

Orsino has called for music while waiting for Feste to arrive and sing him a love-song. The text does not indicate precisely what kind of music is played, but Viola/Cesario's reply to his question, 'How dost thou like this tune?' would suggest that it is a passionate love lament. Orsino's own reference to 'the sweet pangs' of love, spoken while the music is played in the background, would also seem to support this.

It is not necessarily the case, however, that their reactions are identical. Orsino is highly subjective. He is obsessed with his own experience of love: if Cesario ever loves, 'he' is to remember Orsino (the accent falls on the last word of the line, 'In the sweet pangs of it remember *me*'), and Orsino insists, 'For such as *I* am, all true lovers are'. At the same time he sees himself in very conventional terms as the stricken lover who is unstable and unpredictable in everything except his unswerving devotion to his mistress. He is the woebegone lover of the highly wrought sonnets of the sixteenth century, self-indulgent and self-preoccupied despite his almost religious adoration (there are hints of idolatry in the word 'image') of the beloved. He does not merely love; he sees himself loving, in a posture sentimentally hallowed by literature.

Viola/Cesario's reaction is more complex. She is more succinct, but at the same time more richly metaphorical. To her the music seems to be the authentic ('very') echo of the passionate sound which comes from the heart itself. 'the seat/Where love is throned' is a rhetorical elaboration for 'heart', and as such might seem too leisurely and decorative for intense emotion; but it is justified in that it suits the primacy which the music seems to be according to love among the emotions centred on the heart (understood by the Elizabethans to be the source of the emotions). She thus manages to express her deepest feelings, but without reference to her own ego. She focuses on the response evoked by the music, and not, as Orsino does, on herself as the person responding.

Orsino, to do him justice, recognises the eloquence of her reply to his question, but in praising her makes an unconsciously ironic use of the word 'masterly'. Meaning 'like a master', it refers primarily to the sensitivity and skill Viola shows in her use of language. Inevitably, however, it also connotes someone of the male sex – which is appropriate enough in Orsino's own mind, as he believes himself speaking to a boy, but is faintly comic to the audience, aware as it is of Viola's 'Cesario' disguise.

It is on the further implications of this unconscious irony that the succeeding dialogue concentrates. In speculating that Cesario must already have had some experience of love Orsino is nearer the truth than he realises, since he knows neither that he is actually speaking to a woman, nor that that woman has fallen in love with himself. Viola, seeking to be as honest as she can without giving away the secret of her disguise, must choose her words carefully; and she does so (in a way that is highly characteristic of *Twelfth Night*) by playing on Orsino's use of the word 'favour'. For him it means simply that Cesario may have been attracted by a pretty face. Viola's reply, however, is a confession of love for him under the verbal disguise (which, appropriately, corresponds to her physical disguise) of the polite formula, 'by your favour', meaning 'by your leave', but also carrying the implication, 'as a result of your appearance'. A third level of meaning – 'If I were to receive your favour' – may also be present; if so, it further enriches the dramatic complexity of the exchange by seeming to plead for a loving response from Orsino.

The next question, 'What kind of woman is't?' and the answer, 'Of your complexion', puns on the double meaning of 'complexion' as 'looks' and as 'temperament'. Orsino, taking the word in its first meaning, dismisses the putative mistress as not worth Cesario's love since she lacks those delicately pale cheeks which he, along with the conventional sonneteers, considers essential to female beauty; and he is further horrified when told that the anonymous 'she' is about his own age. This causes him to launch into a diatribe against the idea of a woman's marrying a man younger than herself which must strike many modern readers as sexist, though it was commonplace in Shakespeare's time (and probably at any time up to the late twentieth century). What is less usual in his argument is that he maintains that men are much less stable emotionally than women. Orsino's language here becomes very emphatic. The string of epithets, 'giddy', 'unfirm', 'longing', 'wavering', 'sooner lost and worn', suggests a disproportionate strength of feeling which – especially when taken with the similar words 'unstaid' and 'skittish' in line 18 – hints at a disturbing insecurity in Orsino himself. It is not surprising, therefore, that Viola assents in a quietly laconic manner: 'I think it well, my lord'. She agrees, since she fortunately fits the conventional requirement by being younger than Orsino, and perhaps because she herself accepts the orthodox opinion; but such a display of masculine self-

denigration must make her wonder about her ability to hold Orsino's
affection, even if (as seems at this stage highly unlikely) she manages
to win him.

The conclusion of Orsino's argument is that Cesario should choose
a wife younger than himself because otherwise his love for her is
likely to fade. This, again, is bitter-sweet for Viola/Cesario. The
commonplace observation (given a kind of aural underlining which
distinguishes it as 'poetry' by being expressed in a rhyming couplet)
that:

> women are as roses whose fair flower,
> Being once displayed, doth fall that very hour

reminds her acutely of the fragility of her own beauty, which she is
wasting in its prime by denying herself the advantage of showing it in
its proper female context. (This is another side to the comment,
'Disguise, I see thou art a wickedness', II.ii.27, which she had uttered
previously when realising that Olivia had fallen in love with her false
masculine appearance.) The audience feels for her here; and its
sympathy is increased by the heartfelt agreement (again expressed in
a couplet) with which Viola rounds off the discussion:

> And so they are. Alas, that they are so,
> To die, even when they to perfection grow.

For a moment an altogether more sombre note is struck. Not only
are the sexual issues brought to a head in these words, but they also
remind all concerned that human beings are mortal. The antithesis
between 'die' and 'perfection' is a poignant one. The probable
meaning is, not that women die at the point when they reach
perfection, but that, as with the perfect, full-blown rose, the process
of decay sets in precisely at the moment of greatest beauty. To 'grow'
(the last word, one that is foregrounded by the rhyme) implies both
to increase and to decline; it suggests the restlessly undermining
process of time. Thus youth and the threat of age, beauty and the loss
of beauty, vitality and the shadow of decay are simultaneously
present in the one word.

Such hints of darker realities may seem alien to comedy, but it is in
the nature of the special kind of comedy which is to be found in
Twelfth Night that these darker elements are included within it. This
is comedy which requires to be defined not simply in terms of ridicule
and satire, but in terms of an appreciation of the fulfilling richness of
love and life intermingled with an awareness of their fragility and

transience – comedy composed of delicate tensions, which are reflected appropriately in this extract not only in the elegiac touches at its conclusion, but also in the suppressed anxieties and passionately restrained feelings which play beneath the surface of Orsino's dialogue with the disguised Viola. The Duke's own love-melancholy and Viola's witty ambiguities are a source of amusement and delight to the audience, but the tensions of crossed love, heightened by the predicament in which Viola finds herself in her role as 'Cesario', give *Twelfth Night* a more complex tonality. The result is a uniquely Shakespearian blend of irony and passion which evokes both laughter and sympathy.

6 CRITICAL APPROACHES

Early responses to *Twelfth Night* tend to emphasise the gulling of Malvolio. Manningham, for example, who is our only contemporary witness (1602), singles out the 'good practise' of making 'the Stewart believe his Lady widdowe [though Olivia is not a widow] was in love with him'; Leonard Digges in his commendatory verses of 1640 speaks of the theatre being full 'To heare *Molvoglio* that crosse garter'd Gull'; and Charles I, who changed the title of the play in his Folio copy to read 'Malvolio', would seem to have taken much the same view. All these clearly enjoyed what they saw or read. In the Restoration period, however, the diarist, Samuel Pepys, did not share their reaction: on 6 January 1663 he calls the play 'silly'; and on seeing it again, 20 January 1668, he still thinks it 'one of the weakest plays that ever I saw on the stage'. More judiciously, Dr Johnson, in the eighteenth century, observes that it 'is in the graver part elegant and easy, and in some of the lighter scenes exquisitely humorous' (1765) – though it is noteworthy that the characters he mentions for praise are '*Ague-cheek*' and, again, Malvolio. He is somewhat less approving of the play's air of fantasy and improbability, and in particular of Olivia's hasty marriage, which he finds lacking in 'credibility'.

Nineteenth-century critics show a shift in sensibility towards a more emotionally Romantic attitude. The great German Shakespearian, A. W. Schlegel, writes, in 1811, that the comedy unites intrigue 'to a richest fund of comic characters and situations, and the beauteous colours of an ethereal poetry'; and the English critic, William Hazlitt, says that it is 'the most delightful of Shakespear's comedies', and it 'makes us laugh at the follies of mankind, not despise them . . . ' (*Characters of Shakespear's Plays*, 1817). This more sympathetic view also leads to a different interpretation of Malvolio. Charles Lamb, remembering (or, as Sylvan Barnet suggests, *mis*remembering) a moving performance in the part by the actor Robert Bensley, insists that the character should be given 'richness and dignity' and that 'We must not confound him with the eternal old, low steward of comedy'. And in a comment that was to become profoundly influential, he adds: 'I confess that I never saw the catastrophe of this character, while Bensley played it, without a kind of tragic interest' (*Essays of Elia*, 1823).

Nevertheless, for Hazlitt – as for many theatre-goers after him – 'The great and secret charm of *Twelfth Night* is the character of Viola'. In the nineteenth century so strong became the fascination of actresses and audiences with the possibilities for exploitation of Viola's situation as a very feminine being who is compelled to wear unaccustomed male attire that Granville Barker (whose concern was to get back to Elizabethan stage conditions) felt compelled, in 1912, to attack the Victorian tradition, and reaffirm the simple fact that in Shakespeare's theatre it was a boy who played the part of the heroine: 'To that original audience the strain of make-believe in the matter ended just where for us it most begins, at Viola's entrance as a page. Shakespeare's audience saw Cesario without effort as Orsino sees him . . .'

However, there are nineteenth-century critics who also move towards a more integrated view of the play. For example, F. Kreyssig, in 1862, quotes Goethe's saying 'that in every finished work of Shakespeare there could be found a central idea', and uses it as a key to interpreting *Twelfth Night* as a 'series of enamoured situations' extending in an ascending scale from 'the wooing of a charming woman by a feeble-minded, senseless ninnyhammer . . . to the fantastic youthful follies of natures, noble and gifted, to be sure, but untried and still ignorant of their own quality.' E. Montégut (1867) further anticipates twentieth-century criticism in seeing the play as festival comedy – a veritable Twelfth Night charade, which deals both in 'jocund humour' and a kind of beneficent madness. Dream-like follies and extravagances of the imagination interlink the various characters: 'All dream, all are mad, and differ from another only in the kind of their madness'.

This sense of illusion bordering on madness becomes a major theme in modern criticism, though Viola is still singled out for praise because she manages to keep her head in such a frustrating and bewildering world. H. B. Charlton, for example, in *Shakespearian Comedy* (1938), sees the possession of such talent as characteristic both of Shakespeare's heroines generally and Viola in particular. They are women who dominate the comedies by virtue of their balanced perception of the world (decidedly more balanced than that of the men) and their capacity for creative activity in adverse circumstances. J. H. Summers, in 'The Masks of *Twelfth Night*' (1955; reprinted in the Macmillan Casebook), sees all the characters in the play as people wearing masks rather than directly expressing their true selves; and though he inclines towards Charlton's view of Viola as one who causes us to laugh *with* her in her role-playing rather than *at* her, as is most obviously the case with Malvolio, his interest is most strongly focused on the play's deceptive appearances and the false standards which result from such deceptions. D. J. Palmer in 'Art and Nature in *Twelfth Night*' (1967; reprinted in the Macmillan Casebook) takes this interest much further, exploring the pervasive sense of capriciousness and changeableness (as betrayed, for example, in the recurrent motifs of 'time' and 'the sea') which creates a strong impression of nature's instability. Only the art of the play itself, he suggests, holds this at bay; and if we are comically delighted by the confusion, we are also disturbed.

Such awareness of the play's power to create an atmosphere of uncertainty leads inevitably to the feeling that in some respects it is tragic rather than comic. Thus W. H. Auden remarks: 'I have always found the atmosphere of *Twelfth Night* a bit whiffy. I get the impression that Shakespeare wrote the play at a time when he was in no mood for comedy, but in a mood of puritanical aversion to all those pleasing illusions which men cherish and by which they lead their lives' (*The Dyer's Hand*, 1963). Similarly, Clifford Leech, though he distinguishes sharply between proper tragedy and the sense communicated in *Twelfth Night* of 'man's subjection to a relatively kindly pupper-master', pays marked attention to the painful element in Malvolio's humiliation and also finds further 'traces of human suffering' in Sebastian's friend, Antonio (*'Twelfth Night' and Shakespearian Comedy*, 1965).

The knowledge that the play was written at a time when Shakespeare was embarking on his great tragedies perhaps has an undue influence on the view which such critics take, but it is knowledge that cannot be blotted from one's mind. As Patrick Swinden says, Feste rounds off the play with a song of wind and rain, and though he may disappear 'into the warmth and companionship of Olivia's household', we know that what's to come in Shakespeare's subsequent work is 'cold, bare, and tragic' (*An Introduction to Shakespeare's Comedies*, 1973). *Twelfth Night* is overshadowed by our consciousness of this; it becomes a mingled skein of many different kinds of comedy, producing what E. A. J. Honigmann, in his 'Introduction' to the Macmillan edition (1972), calls 'painful comedy'.

There is, nonetheless, an important countervailing stream in modern criticism which reminds us of the positive standards embodied in the comedy of *Twelfth Night*. This is exemplified by the approaches of John Russell Brown and C. L. Barber in two influential books written in the late 1950s. In *Shakespeare and his Comedies* (1957) Brown argues that the positive and negative aspects of three major themes – love's wealth, love's truth, and the orderly/disorderly power of love – are set in constructive opposition to one another, with the ultimate effect of supporting a vision of love which is life-enhancing. Barber, as the title of his book suggests (*Shakespeare's Festive Comedies*, 1959), takes up Montégut's idea of festivity and expands it into a general principle of Shakespearian comedy. With regard to *Twelfth Night* in particular, he maintains that 'What enables Viola to bring off her role in disguise is her perfect courtesy' – 'courtesy' meaning, not merely politeness, but command of the style and manners appropriate to all social situations, a relaxed adaptability and flexibility indicative of innate gentility. This gives her the festive spirit which enables her to enjoy life, and which fundamentally she shares with Sir Toby and the other 'misrule' characters in Olivia's household. Kill-joy Malvolio, on the other hand, is 'hostile to holiday' and unable therefore to take part in the comedy's affirmative celebration.

Alexander Leggatt (*Shakespeare's Comedy of Love*, 1974) adopts a somewhat different approach in that he sees a structural division in the play between its prose and its poetry, and a corresponding division between comic (or low-life) and romantic characters. To be divided in this way implies isolation: Orsino and Olivia are isolated and trapped by their attitudinised postures of love, and the comic characters, Malvolio especially, are similarly restricted by their 'limited, clearly defined comic personalities'. For Leggatt (as for H. B. Charlton), the admirable counterpoise to such rigidity is to be found in the flexibility of Viola, whose virtue is to be able to make these isolating barriers fall.

Ruth Nevo, in one of the more intelligent recent studies of Shakespearian comedy, *Comic Transformations in Shakespeare* (1980), also gives positive status to Viola as a character capable of releasing creative energy; but her way of working this out is different again. In Nevo's view, Olivia, who cannot respond to Orsino because of his lack of assertive masculinity, finds her frustrated sexual feeling aroused by the pert boyishness of Viola/Cesario, while the essential femininity of Viola, making itself felt even beneath the mask of 'Cesario', enables Orsino in the course of their relationship to develop 'a new, mature and manly good sense'. Nevo is also virtually the only critic to praise the vigorous masculinity of Sebastian; to her he is the true counterpart of his sister in representing the creative energy which is the driving force of the comedy, and which shows a way out of its baffling postures.

This positive role is once more attributed to Viola by Karen Greif in her study of 'Plays and Playing in *Twelfth Night*' (1981; reprinted in '*Twelfth Night*': *Critical Essays*, ed. Wells), but her primary theme is the ambiguity caused by the proliferation of adopted or imposed roles in this play – a comic device which has its precedents in Shake-speare's earlier plays, but which in *Twelfth Night* is carried further than ever before. Greif's conclusion is that 'In a comic world devoted to playing and yet mirroring the actual world of being . . .no permanent resolution of these ambiguities is ever possible. Shake-speare himself shrugs off the task of providing any final illumination with delightful finesse.'

This open-ended conclusion is also perhaps the only one that can safely be drawn from study of the play and its critics. No single approach has so far yielded a completely satisfactory interpretation, and no critic has pronounced the perfect judgement upon it. Whether *Twelfth Night* should be regarded as corrective moral comedy or pure hedonistic fantasy; whether it is to be seen as optimistic in mood or shaded by incipient tragedy; whether all its characters deserve sympathy or whether Olivia and Orsino, for example, deserve mockery for their romantic sentimentality and Malvolio and Sir Andrew ridicule for their pretentious egoism – these are all questions on which some light has been shed, but which cannot be said to have been answered definitively. Each reader – or better, each member of the theatre audience – is still left to decide the precise quality of the balance in this poised and elusive play for himself/herself. Criticism helps towards an appreciation of the richness of its elements, but their distribution and combination remains, and will probably always remain, a matter for the judgement of each sensitive and discriminating individual.

REVISION QUESTIONS

1. Charles I re-titled the play, 'Malvolio'. Is Malvolio the dominant character? If not, who is? Or is it impossible to single out one such character? Discuss the implications of all these questions.

2. 'Disguise, I see thou art a wickedness.' (II.ii.27)

   Why does Viola say this? What are the reasons for her adopting the guise of 'Cesario'? What advantages and disadvantages does it prove to have for her? What dramatic effects does Shakespeare manage to achieve by means of this disguise?

3. 'For such as I am, all true lovers are.' (II.iv.17)

   Is Orsino a representative lover? What do his speeches tell us about his attitude to love? What do we learn from other characters in the play about the quality of his love for Olivia?

4. Compare Viola and Sebastian. What influence do they have respectively on the action of the play?

5. Consider Maria's sketch of Malvolio's character at II.iii.151–8 ('The devil a Puritan that he is . . . and on that vice in him will my revenge find notable cause to work.') Are her comments borne out by the things Malvolio does and says in the rest of the play? Is what she says the whole truth about him, or what else must be taken into account?

6. Olivia has several wooers, or would-be wooers – Orsino, Malvolio, Sir Andrew, Sebastian. Cesario is also a proxy wooer, and Olivia would like 'him' to be a genuine wooer on 'his' own

behalf. Compare the ways in which these characters conduct their wooing, and/or the ways in which they think of her in relation to themselves, either in soliloquy or in dialogue with other characters.

7. Examine the comments which are made within the play on the role of Feste as a Fool, including those made by Feste himself. What do *you* consider to be his role?

8. 'Dost thou think, because thou art virtuous, there shall be no more cakes and ale?' (II.iii.117–19)

    What does Sir Toby's retort to Malvolio tell us about his values compared with Malvolio's? How is the opposition between the two developed in the play?

9. It has been suggested that there is only a loose relationship between the Orsino–Olivia–Viola–Sebastian group and the Sir Toby–Maria–Fabian–Feste–Malvolio group. Do you agree? Why do you think Shakespeare added the latter group to the story he derived from his sources?

10. Consider the effects Shakespeare achieves by alternating poetry and prose from one scene to another, and within the same scene.

11. How does Shakespeare play off the wider knowledge of his audience against the more limited knowledge of his characters – for example, with regard to the identity of Viola and the survival of Sebastian?

12. What atmospheric effects does Shakespeare achieve by means of music and song? Compare the themes and styles of the songs in II.iii ('O mistress mine! Where are you roaming?'), II.iv ('Come away, come away, death') and V.i ('When that I was and a little tiny boy').

13. Consider the importance of the pun, and of word-play generally, in *Twelfth Night*.

14. 'I do not now fool myself, to let imagination jade me; for every reason excites me to this, that my lady loves me.' (Malvolio, II.v.164–6)

'... I am ready to distrust mine eyes,
And wrangle with my reason that persuades me
To any other trust but that I am mad –
Or else the lady's mad.' (Sebastian, IV.ii.13–16)

Discuss the use made of deceptions and self-deceptions in *Twelfth Night*.

15. 'Shakespeare's *Twelfth Night* is a holiday entertainment in which we are made aware of the proximity of the non-holiday world.' (M. M. Mahood)

   Discuss the light-hearted, festive elements in the play, and compare them with its darker, more realistic moments.

16. 'The happiness of the lovers would seem to have been bought at a price which excludes Malvolio, and we may feel that this circumscribes and diminishes the final effect of their happiness.' (G. K. Hunter)

   Do you find a fundamental discordance in the ending of *Twelfth Night*?

17. '*Twelfth Night* is a collection of self-borrowings' (Patrick Swinden). How does Shakespeare re-present and reshape his previous comedies in this play?

18. 'Shakespeareans are divided, it is well known, into three classes, those who prefer to read Shakespeare in the book, those who prefer to see him acted on the stage, and those who run perpetually from book to stage gathering plunder.' (Virginia Woolf) What difference do you think there might be between reading *Twelfth Night* and seeing it acted on stage, or television? (Draw on any productions that you may have seen.)

APPENDIX:
SHAKESPEARE'S THEATRE
BY HAROLD BROOKS

We should speak, as Muriel Bradbrook reminds us, not of the Elizabethan stage but of Elizabethan stages. Plays of Shakespeare were acted on tour, in the halls of mansions, one at least in Gray's Inn, frequently at Court, and after 1609 at the Blackfriars, a small roofed theatre for those who could afford the price. But even after his Company acquired the Blackfriars, we know of no play of his not acted (unless, rather improbably, *Troilus* is an exception) for the general public at the Globe, or before 1599 at its predecessor, The Theatre, which, since the Globe was constructed from the same timbers, must have resembled it. Describing the Globe, we can claim therefore to be describing, in an acceptable sense, Shakespeare's theatre, the physical structure his plays were designed to fit. Even in the few probably written for a first performance elsewhere, adaptability to that structure would be in his mind.

For the facilities of the Globe we have evidence from the drawing of the Swan theatre (based on a sketch made by a visitor to London about 1596) which depicts the interior of another public theatre; the builder's contract for the Fortune theatre, which in certain respects (fortunately including the dimensions and position of the stage) was to copy the Globe; indications in the dramatic texts; comments, like Ben Jonson's on the throne let down from above by machinery; and eye-witness testimony to the number of spectators (in round figures, 3000) accommodated in the auditorium.

In communicating with the audience, the actor was most favourably placed. Soliloquising at the centre of the front of the great platform, he was at the mid-point of the theatre, with no one among the spectators more than sixty feet away from him. That platform-stage (Figs I and II) was the most important feature for performance at the Globe. It had the audience – standing in the yard (10) and seated in the galleries (9) – on three sides of it. It was 43 feet wide, and $27\frac{1}{2}$ feet from front to back. Raised ($5\frac{1}{2}$ feet) above the level of the yard, it had a trap-door (II.8) giving access to the space below it. The

SHAKESPEARE'S THEATRE

The stage and its adjuncts; the tiring-house; and the auditorium.

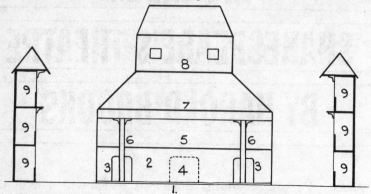

FIG I ELEVATION

1. Platform stage (approximately five feet above the ground) 2. Tiring-house
3. Tiring-house doors to stage 4. Conjectured third door 5. Tiring-house
gallery (balustrade and partitioning not shown) 6. Pillars supporting the
heavens 7. The heavens 8. The hut 9. The spectators' galleries

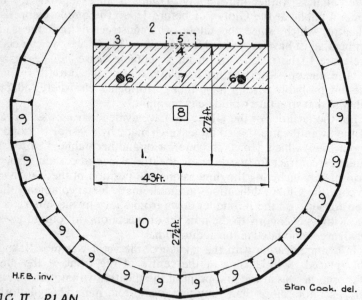

H.F.B. inv.

Stan Cook. del.

FIG II PLAN

1. Platform stage 2. Tiring-house 3. Tiring-house doors to stage
4. Conjectural third door 5. Conjectural discovery space (alternatively behind 3)
6. Pillars supporting the heavens 7. The heavens 8. Trap door 9. Spectators'
gallery 10. The yard

The Globe

An artist's imaginative recreation of a typical Elizabethan theatre

actors, with their equipment, occupied the 'tiring house' (attiring house: 2) immediately at the back of the stage. The stage-direction 'within' means inside the tiring-house. Along its frontage, probably from the top of the second storey, juts out the canopy or 'Heavens', carried on two large pillars rising through the platform (6, 7) and sheltering the rear part of the stage, the rest of which, like the yard, was open to the sky. If the 'hut' (1.8) housing the machinery for descents, stood, as in the Swan drawing, above the 'Heavens', that covering must have had a trap-door, so that the descents could be made through it.

Descents are one illustration of the vertical dimension the dramatist could use to supplement the playing-area of the great platform. The other opportunities are provided by the tiring-house frontage or facade. About this facade the evidence is not so complete or clear as we should like, so that Fig. 1 is in part conjectural. Two doors giving entry to the platform there certainly were (3). A third (4) is probable but not certain. When curtained, a door, most probably this one, would furnish what must be termed a discovery-space (II.5), not an inner stage (on which action in any depth would have been out of sight for a significant part of the audience). Usually no more than two actors were revealed (exceptionally, three), who often then moved out on to the platform. An example of this is Ferdinand and Miranda in *The Tempest* 'discovered' at chess, then seen on the platform speaking with their fathers. Similarly the gallery (1.5) was not an upper stage. Its use was not limited to the actors: sometimes it functioned as 'lords' rooms' for favoured spectators, sometimes, perhaps, as a musicians' gallery. Frequently the whole gallery would not be needed for what took place aloft: a window-stage (as in the first balcony scene in *Romeo*, even perhaps in the second) would suffice. Most probably this would be a part (at one end) of the gallery itself; or just possibly, if the gallery did not (as it does in the Swan drawing) extend the whole width of the tiring-house, a window in the left or right-hand door. As the texts show, whatever was presented aloft, or in the discovery-space, was directly related to the action on the platform, so that at no time was there left, between the audience and the action of the drama, a great bare space of platform-stage. In relating Shakespeare's drama to the physical conditions of the theatre, the primacy of that platform is never to be forgotton.

Note: The present brief account owes most to C. Walter Hodges, *The Globe Restored*; Richard Hosley in *A New Companion to Shakespeare Studies*, and in *The Revels History of English Drama*; and to articles by Hosley and Richard Southern in *Shakespeare Survey*, 12, 1959, where full discussion can be found.

HAROLD BROOKS

FURTHER READING

AND

REFERENCES

Editions

Honigmann, E. A. J. (ed.) *Twelfth Night* (London: Macmillan, 1972)
The Macmillan Shakespeare. [This is the text used in the present
commentary.]

Furness, Horace Howard (ed.) *Twelfth Night* (Philadelphia and
London: Lippincott, 1901) New Variorum Edition.

Lothian, J. M. and Craik, T. W. (eds) *Twelfth Night* (London:
Methuen, 1975) The Arden Edition of the Works of William
Shakespeare.

Mahood, M. M. (ed.) *Twelfth Night* (Harmondsworth: Penguin
Books, 1968) The New Penguin Shakespeare.

Background and sources

Badawi, M. M., *Background to Shakespeare* (London: Macmillan,
1981).

Bullough, Geoffrey, *Narrative and Dramatic Sources of Shakespeare*
(London: Routledge & Kegan Paul, 1958) vol. II, *The Comedies,
1597–1603*.

Chambers, E. K., *A Short Life of Shakespeare*, with the sources,
abridged by Charles Williams, from *William Shakespeare: A Study
of Facts and Problems* (Oxford: Clarendon Press, 1933).

Wells, Stanley (ed.) *The Cambridge Companion to Shakespeare
Studies* (Cambridge: Cambridge University Press, 1986).

Collections of comments, essays, and extracts from critical works

King, Walter N. (ed.) *Twentieth Century Interpretations of Twelfth
Night* (Englewood Cliffs, New Jersey: Prentice-Hall, 1968).

Palmer, D. J. (ed.) *Shakespeare: 'Twelfth Night', A Casebook* (London: Macmillan, 1972) Macmillan Casebook Series.
Wells, Stanley (ed.) *Twelfth Night: Critical Essays* (New York and London: Garland, 1986).

Other studies

Auden, W. H., *The Dyer's Hand* (London: Faber & Faber, 1973).
Barber, C. L., *Shakespeare's Festive Comedy* (Princeton: Princeton University Press, 1959).
Brown, John Russell, *Shakespeare and his Comedies* (London: Methuen, 1957).
Charlton, H. B., *Shakespearian Comedy* (London: Methuen, 1938).
Gregson, J. M., *Shakespeare: Twelfth Night* (London: Arnold, 1980) Studies in English Literature Series.
Hotson, Leslie, *The First Night of Twelfth Night* (London: Rupert Hart-Davies, 1954).
Leech, Clifford, *'Twelfth Night' and Shakespearian Comedy* (Toronto: University of Toronto Press, 1965).
Leggatt, Alexander, *Shakespeare's Comedy of Love* (London: Methuen, 1974).
Nevo, Ruth, *Comic Transformations in Shakespeare* (London, Methuen, 1980).
Swinden, Patrick, *An Introduction to Shakespeare's Comedies* (London: Macmillan, 1973).

Mastering English Literature
Richard Gill

Mastering English Literature will help readers both to enjoy English Literature and to be successful in 'O' levels, 'A' levels and other public exams. It is an introduction to the study of poetry, novels and drama which helps the reader in four ways - by providing ways of approaching literature, by giving examples and practice exercises, by offering hints on how to write about literature, and by the author's own evident enthusiasm for the subject. With extracts from more than 200 texts, this is an enjoyable account of how to get the maximum satisfaction out of reading, whether it be for formal examinations or simply for pleasure.

Work Out English Literature ('A' level)
S.H. Burton

This book familiarises 'A' level English Literature candidates with every kind of test which they are likely to encounter. Suggested answers are worked out step by step and accompanied by full author's commentary. The book helps students to clarify their aims and establish techniques and standards so that they can make appropriate responses to similar questions when the examination pressures are on. It opens up fresh ways of looking at the full range of set texts, authors and critical judgements and motivates students to know more of these matters.

MACMILLAN SHAKESPEARE VIDEO WORKSHOPS

DAVID WHITWORTH

Three unique book and video packages, each examining a particular aspect of Shakespeare's work; tragedy, comedy and the Roman plays. Designed for all students of Shakespeare, each package assumes no previous knowledge of the plays and can serve as a useful introduction to Shakespeare for 'O' and 'A' level candidates as well as for students at colleges and institutes of further, higher and adult education.

The material is based on the New Shakespeare Company Workshops at the Roundhouse, adapted and extended for television. By combining the resources of television and a small theatre company, this exploration of Shakespeare's plays offers insights into varied interpretations, presentation, styles of acting as well as useful background information.

While being no substitute for seeing the whole plays in performance, it is envisaged that these video cassettes will impart something of the original excitement of the theatrical experience, and serve as a welcome complement to textual analysis leading to an enriched and broader view of the plays.

Each package consists of:

* the Macmillan Shakespeare editions of the plays concerned;

* a video cassette available in VHS or Beta;

* a leaflet of teacher's notes.

THE TORTURED MIND
looks at the four tragedies Hamlet, Othello, Macbeth and King Lear.

THE COMIC SPIRIT
examines the comedies Much Ado About Nothing, Twelfth Night, A Midsummer Night's Dream, and As You Like It.

THE ROMAN PLAYS
Features Julius Caesar, Antony and Cleopatra
and Coriolanus